ANXIETY RELEASED

A JOURNEY THROUGH TRIGGERS, PANIC, AND PROGRESS, MASTER MINDFULNESS & RELAXATION THROUGH COPING TECHNIQUES AND EXPOSURE THERAPY TO HELP RELIEVE ANXIOUS THOUGHTS

OLIVIA J PATTERSON

Olivia J Patterson

COPYRIGHT

© Copyright Higher Level Publishing 2024 - All rights reserved.

The content within this book may not be reproduced, duplicated or transmitted without direct written permission from the author or the publisher.

Under no circumstances will any blame or legal responsibility be held against the publisher, or author, for any damages, reparation, or monetary loss due to the information contained within this book. Either directly or indirectly. You are responsible for your own choices, actions, and results.

Legal Notice:

This book is copyright-protected. This book is only for personal use. You cannot amend, distribute, sell, use, quote or paraphrase any part, of the content within this book, without the consent of the author or publisher.

Disclaimer Notice:

Please note the information contained within this document is for educational and entertainment purposes only. All effort has been expended to present accurate, up-to-date, and reliable, complete information. No warranties of any kind are declared or implied. Readers acknowledge that the author is not engaging in the rendering of legal, financial, medical or professional advice. The content within this book has been derived from various sources. Please consult a licensed professional before attempting any techniques outlined in this book.

By reading this document, the reader agrees that under no circumstances is the author responsible for any losses, direct or indirect, which are incurred as a result of the use of the information contained within this document, including, but not limited to, — errors, omissions, or inaccuracies.

TABLE OF CONTENTS

Introduction	ix
1. UNDERSTANDING ANXIETY	1
What is Anxiety?	1
Symptoms of Anxiety:	2
Types of Anxiety Disorders:	2
The Anxiety Cycle	3
Causes of Anxiety	4
Anxiety vs. Stress	7
The Role of Evolution	8
Reflecting on Your Progress:	10
2. THE ANXIOUS BRAIN	12
The Neuroscience of Anxiety	12
Neurotransmitters and Anxiety	13
The Fight, Flight, or Freeze Response	14
How Anxiety Affects Your Thinking	15
How Anxiety Affects Behaviour:	16
The Anxiety-Sleep Connection	17
The Role of Genetics:	17
Reflecting on Your Progress:	18
3. IDENTIFYING YOUR ANXIETY TRIGGERS:	20
What Are Anxiety Triggers?	20
Common Anxiety Triggers :	21
The Anxiety Journal:	23
Recognizing Thought Patterns:	25
The Role of Avoidance:	27
Creating a Trigger Hierarchy:	30
Reflecting on Your Progress:	31
4. CHALLENGING ANXIOUS THOUGHTS:	33
Understanding Cognitive Distortions:	33
The Power of Thought Records:	35
Socratic Questioning:	37

Mindfulness and Acceptance:	40
Reflecting on Your Progress:	44

5. UNDERSTANDING AND MANAGING PANIC ATTACKS ... 46
   - What is a Panic Attack? ... 46
   - The Physiology of Panic Attacks ... 47
   - Common Triggers for Panic Attacks: ... 47
   - The Panic Cycle ... 48
   - Strategies for Managing Panic Attacks: ... 50
   - Preventing Panic Attacks: ... 52
   - When to Seek Professional Help ... 54
   - *Reflecting on Your Progress* ... 54

6. MINDFULNESS AND ANXIETY ... 56
   - Introduction to Mindfulness ... 56
   - The Science Behind Mindfulness ... 57
   - Mindfulness in Daily Life ... 60
   - Mindfulness for Anxious Thoughts: ... 61
     - ▫ Random memories: ... 63
   - Loving-Kindness Meditation ... 63
   - *Reflecting on Your Progress* ... 65

7. LIFESTYLE CHANGES FOR ANXIETY MANAGEMENT ... 69
   - Sleep Hygiene ... 69
   - Time Management and Productivity ... 73
   - *Interactive Element 4: Priority Planner* ... 74
   - Creating an Anxiety-Friendly Environment ... 77
   - *Reflecting on Your Progress:* ... 78

8. RELAXATION TECHNIQUES ... 80
   - The Science of Relaxation ... 80
   - Progressive Muscle Relaxation (PMR) ... 82
   - Creating a Relaxation Routine ... 88
   - Reflecting on Your Progress ... 89

9. EXPOSURE THERAPY ... 91
   - Understanding Exposure Therapy ... 91
   - Types of Exposure Therapy ... 92
   - Creating an Exposure Hierarchy ... 93
   - Implementing Exposure Exercises ... 94
   - Coping with discomfort during exposure ... 96

Overcoming Common Challenges in Exposure Therapy	96
Celebrating Success and Maintaining Progress	98
When to Seek Professional Help	99
Reflecting on Your Progress	100

10. ANXIETY IN SPECIFIC SITUATIONS — 102
Social Anxiety	102
Performance Anxiety	104
Health Anxiety	106
Financial Anxiety	109
Travel Anxiety	110
Test and Exam Anxiety	111
Relationship Anxiety	112
Generalized Anxiety in Daily Life	114
Reflecting on Your Progress	115

11. WHEN TO SEEK PROFESSIONAL HELP — 117
Recognizing when professional help is needed	117
Types of mental health professionals	119
Types of therapy for anxiety	121
Medication options for anxiety	123
Reflecting on your progress:	128

12. MAINTAINING PROGRESS AND PREVENTING RELAPSE — 130
Understanding the nature of recovery	130
Creating a maintenance plan	132
Relapse prevention strategies	134
Recognizing and managing setbacks	136
The Role of Ongoing Self-Education	137
Celebrating Progress and Success	138
Strategies for building resilience:	140
Reflecting on your progress:	141

13. CELEBRATING PROGRESS AND ACKNOWLEDGING ACHIEVEMENTS — 143
The Importance of Acknowledging Progress	143
Overcoming the Tendency to Dismiss Progress	144
Identifying and Celebrating Small Wins	145
Measuring Progress Over Time:	147
Celebrating Achievements:	148

Dealing with Setbacks	149
The Role of Self-Compassion:	150
Setting Future Goals	151
SMART Objective Example:	152
14. INTEGRATING ANXIETY MANAGEMENT INTO DAILY LIFE	155
Creating an Anxiety Friendly Routine	155
Micro-Practices for Anxiety Management	156
Strategies for workplace anxiety management:	158
Anxiety Management in Relationships	159
Technology and Anxiety Management	160
Managing Anxiety During Major Life Changes	161
Creating an Anxiety-Management Emergency Kit	163
Reflecting on Your Anxiety Management Journey	165
Conclusion:	168
Chapter References	175

FREE ANXIETY JOURNAL GIFT - PRINT

Scan the QR Code Below to Download your FREE Anxiety Journal

https://anxietyjournal.higherlevelpublishing.com/

INTRODUCTION

Welcome to Anxiety Released: This is "Your Anxiety Mastery Roadmap." In a world of trials, tribulations, tears, joy and happiness, feelings that often feel overwhelming, you have taken the first crucial step towards reclaiming control of your life from the stressful and pressured feelings of anxiety. This book will be your comprehensive guide to understanding, managing, and ultimately mastering your feelings of anxiety.

Anxiety is a universal human experience; everyone feels it at some time, some less or more than others, but when it begins to interfere with your daily life, relationships, and personal growth, you know it's time to take action. Whether you're dealing with generalized anxiety, social anxiety, panic attacks, or specific phobias, this book offers targeted, proven strategies to address your particular anxiety needs and challenges.

In the following chapters, we'll embark on the journey together. We'll explore the roots of anxiety, delve into the science behind it, and most importantly, equip you with practical, evidence-based tools to manage it effectively so that you can feel better. We will look at cognitive restructuring techniques, mindfulness practices, life-

INTRODUCTION

style changes, and even exposure therapy. You'll gain a diverse toolkit of strategies that will help not only calm your mind but also help you regain control.

One thing to remember is that managing anxiety is not about eliminating it – it's about building resilience, developing coping strategies, and creating a life where anxiety doesn't interfere or has the power to hold you back from pursuing your goals and enjoying your life experiences.

As you work and progress through this book, please be patient with yourself. Change takes time, and each person's journey with anxiety is specific and unique. Celebrate all your small victories, the big ones too. Learn from setbacks, and keep moving forward step by step.

You have the strength within you to quiet the chaos of anxiety and lead a more anxiety-controlled, peaceful, and fulfilling life.

Let's begin this transformative journey together. Your roadmap to anxiety mastery starts here.

Below are a few suggestions; choosing any will help you get the most out of "Anxiety Released: Your Anxiety Mastery Roadmap."

1. Read Sequentially: The chapters are designed to build upon each other, providing a comprehensive approach to anxiety management, so it will be more beneficial to go through the book and the chapters in the order it is written. Trust me it will all make sense.

2. Engage with Interactive Elements: You will see that each chapter includes exercises, self-assessments, and practical tools. Do take the time to complete these, as they're crucial for applying what you've just learned and will apply to your unique situation.

3. Keep a Journal: Use a dedicated notebook to record your thoughts, experiences, and progress as you work through the book. Purchase these items specifically and choose items that you enjoy using.

INTRODUCTION

4. Practice Regularly: Anxiety management is a skill you must practice, and as you practice, you will be able to improve and implement it when needed. As you learn, try incorporating the steps and techniques into your daily life.

5. Be Patient and Compassionate: Remember, progress isn't always straightforward, there will be fits and starts as you go along and get used to the methods and strategies. Be kind to yourself as you learn and grow.

6. Revisit Chapters: Feel free to return to and revisit chapters if needed. Some concepts may resonate more deeply as you progress, and clarity is always good.

7. Seek Support: Consider sharing your journey with a trusted friend, family member, or professional who can give an understanding ear. Support can be invaluable in this process.

8. Customize Your Approach: Only some strategies will work for everyone. Feel free to focus and practice the techniques that resonate most with you. If you feel it isn't working, try another method.

Let's begin our journey to mastering anxiety.

CHAPTER 1
UNDERSTANDING ANXIETY

WHAT IS ANXIETY?

"Imagine your brain as a highly sensitive car alarm. Sometimes it goes off when there's real danger, such as a potential thief tugging at the car door. But there are those other times when it blares when a leaf brushes against the windshield. Both situations will give you the same level of anxious feelings. One is a perceived threat and one is not. This is anxiety in a nutshell."

Definition: Anxiety is a normal human emotion characterized by worry, nervousness, or unease, typically about an imminent event or something with an uncertain outcome.

Protective function: Anxiety serves as our body's natural alert system, preparing us to respond to potential threats, also known as "the fight or flight response."

Anxiety vs. Anxiety Disorders: While occasional anxiety is normal, anxiety disorders involve persistent, excessive worry that gets in the way and interferes with daily life.

SYMPTOMS OF ANXIETY:

Physical: Racing heart, sweating, trembling, nausea, shortness of breath, IBS

Emotional: Fear, dread, restlessness, irritability, heightened emotions

Cognitive: Racing thoughts, difficulty concentrating, negative thinking, constant worry

Interactive Element: Anxiety Check-In

How often have you experienced the following in the past two weeks? (give each question a score)

0 = Never, 1 = Sometimes, 2 = Often, 3 = Almost always

1. Feeling nervous, anxious, or on edge ___
2. Not being able to stop or control worrying. ___
3. Worrying too much about different things ___
4. Trouble relaxing ___
5. Being so restless that it's hard to sit still ___
6. Becoming easily annoyed or irritable ___
7. Feeling afraid as if something awful might happen ___

Total: ___

Scoring: 0-4: Minimal anxiety 5-9: Mild anxiety 10-14: Moderate anxiety 15-21: Severe anxiety

Note: This is a simplified version of the GAD-7 scale. It's not a diagnostic tool that can help you to gauge your anxiety levels.

TYPES OF ANXIETY DISORDERS:

Generalized Anxiety Disorder (GAD): Persistent and excessive worry about various aspects of life. Example: Sarah constantly worries about her job, finances, health, and family, even when things are going well.

- Panic Disorder: Recurrent unexpected panic attacks and fear of future attacks. Example: Tom experiences sudden episodes of intense fear accompanied by physical symptoms like a racing heart and shortness of breath, often in situations where others wouldn't feel afraid.
- Social Anxiety Disorder: Intense fear of social situations and being judged by others. Example: Emma avoids social gatherings and speaking up in meetings due to an overwhelming fear of embarrassment.
- Specific Phobias are intense fears of a particular object or situation. For example, despite living on the 20th floor, John takes the stairs daily due to his intense fear of elevators.
- Obsessive-Compulsive Disorder (OCD): Recurring, intrusive thoughts (obsessions) leading to repetitive behaviours (compulsions). Example: Maria feels compelled to check if she's locked the door multiple times before leaving home, fearing burglary if she doesn't.
- Post-Traumatic Stress Disorder (PTSD): Anxiety following exposure to a traumatic event. Example: After surviving a car accident, David experiences flashbacks and avoids driving.

THE ANXIETY CYCLE

"Think of anxiety like a merry-go-round that spins faster and faster. Let's hop on and see how it works:"

- **Trigger**: An event, thought, or situation that initiates anxiety.
- **Physical Sensations**: The body's fight-or-flight response activates (e.g., increased heart rate).
- **Misinterpretation**: These physical sensations are often misinterpreted as dangerous.
- **Catastrophic Thinking**: The mind jumps to worst-case scenarios.

- **Avoidance Behaviours**: To reduce anxiety, the person avoids the trigger.
- **Reinforcement**: Avoidance provides temporary relief, reinforcing the cycle.

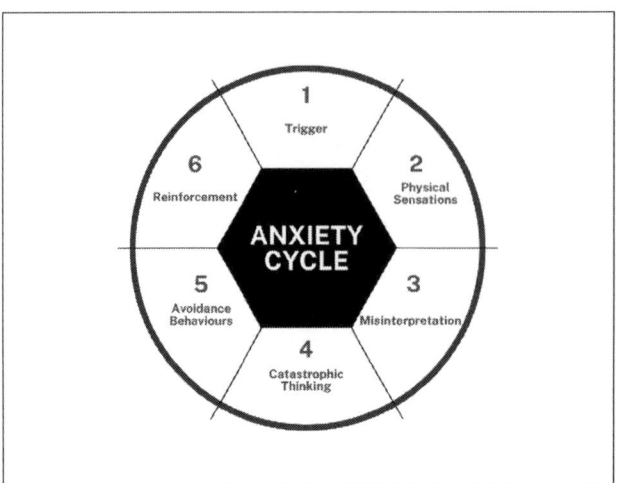

Journal Prompt: "Reflect on a recent anxious experience. Can you identify each stage of the cycle?"

CAUSES OF ANXIETY

Anxiety is like a fairy complicated recipe, each person does (experiences) it a little differently, and each ingredient has a role to play in the result.

Biological Factors:

Genetics: Anxiety can sometimes run in families, suggesting that there may be a genetic link. Studies carried out on twins have shown that if one identical twin has an anxiety disorder, the other has a 30-40% chance of developing an anxiety disorder as well. However, genetics isn't destiny. Environmental factors inevitably interact with genetic predispositions, a concept known as gene-environment interaction.

Brain Chemistry: Neurotransmitters play a crucial role in the development of anxiety.

For example:

- Serotonin helps to regulate mood, sleep, and appetite. Low levels of serotonin are associated with anxiety and depression.
- Norepinephrine increases alertness and arousal, potentially contributing to anxiety when levels are imbalanced.
- GABA (Gamma-Amino-butyric Acid) is an inhibitory neurotransmitter that can help calm your anxiety when activated.
- Dopamine, while this is often associated with pleasure, can also contribute to anxiety levels when the Dopamine levels are disturbed.

Environmental Factors:

Trauma: Traumatic experiences can significantly impact anxiety levels.

This could include a host of different reasons:

- Childhood abuse or neglect
- Witnessing violence
- Experiencing a natural disaster
- Being in an accident
- Military combat exposure

Trauma can alter the brain's structure and function, particularly in areas like the amygdala (fear centre) and the hippocampus (memory processing area), leading to heightened anxiety responses.

Chronic stress can contribute to anxiety in several ways:

- It keeps the body in a constant state of high alert, wearing down physical and mental resources.

- Prolonged exposure to the stress hormones like cortisol can affect both brain structure and the brain's function.
- Stress can lead to unhealthy coping mechanisms (like substance use) that may make symptoms of anxiety worse.
- Significant life changes, even positive ones like getting married or starting a new job, can be significant stressors.
- Moving home or to a new area can impact stress levels negatively.

There are times when anxiety can be Learned behaviour through:

- **Observational learning**: Children may learn anxious behaviours by watching anxious parents.
- **Classical conditioning**: A neutral stimulus becomes associated with anxiety after repeated pairing with an anxiety-provoking situation.
- **Negative experiences**: A bad experience (like public embarrassment) can lead to anxiety in similar future situations.
- *Personality Traits:* Certain personality traits can mean that individuals are more likely to develop feelings of anxiety:
- **Perfectionism**: Setting unrealistically high standards can lead to constant worry about meeting these standards. Failing to meet those standards will intensify the feelings of fear.
- **Need for control**: When faced with uncertainty or lack of power, anxiety can increase, leaving you feeling powerless and sometimes out of control.
- **Neuroticism**: A tendency towards negative emotions can amplify anxiety responses, often, this comes along with negative self-talk.
- **Introversion**: While not inherently linked to anxiety, introverts may find certain social situations more challenging, potentially leading to social anxiety and a lack of confidence.

- **Sensitivity**: Highly sensitive individuals may be more prone to overstimulation and anxiety.

These traits aren't inherently negative, but when extreme, they can contribute to anxiety disorders. Understanding one's personality can be a step towards managing anxiety more effectively. When situations occur that make you feel anxious, step back and try to identify precisely how you are feeling. This will bring you closer to managing your feelings and the situation's outcome.

ANXIETY VS. STRESS

While some do not know the difference between anxiety and stress, these words are often used interchangeably, but they each have their distinct characteristics:

Stress:

- It is typically a response to an external cause (e.g., a work deadline)
- A work meeting is scheduled to take place.
- Usually, it subsides once the situation is resolved.
- Can be positive (eustress: a positive and beneficial form of stress where endorphins are released) or negative (distress: extreme anxiety, which can cause physical pain symptoms and is known to have a negative impact on the body.)
- Often involves feelings of overwhelm, irritability, and fatigue.

Anxiety:

- Can occur without an apparent external trigger; sometimes our thoughts take over and our anxiety levels may rise without external factors being involved.
- Often persists even when the stressor is gone and the body stays in the fight or flight mode for some time.

- Is characterized by persistent worry about future events and this can make worse the feelings of anxiety.
- Frequently involves feelings of apprehension and dread. A feeling of uncertainty and fear can also accompany this emotion.

Interaction between stress and anxiety:

- Chronic stress can lead to anxiety disorders, which can be long-term and impact health and mental well-being.
- Anxiety can make individuals more susceptible to stress and all the negative issues that surround stress, such as heart attacks, strokes, and sleep issues, to name a few.
- Both can cause similar physical symptoms (e.g., muscle tension, rapid heartbeat)

Examples:

- Stress: Feeling the stress of making a speech or presentation.
- Anxiety: Worrying excessively about the presentation or speech well before the event and imagining all the things that could go wrong.

THE ROLE OF EVOLUTION

Anxiety used as a survival mechanism:

- In prehistoric times, a long time ago, anxiety helped our ancestors stay alert to potential dangers (such as predators)
- The fight-or-flight response, triggered by anxiety, prepared the body for quick action. Whether they should get ready to fight or get ready for flight (run)
- Worrying and planning for future threats increased the chances of survival. Thinking about how you will react or

behave in certain situations increases the probability of things working out in your favour.

Why our brains are wired for anxiety:

- The amygdala, often called the brain's "fear centre", can trigger anxiety responses before conscious awareness. Have you ever been on a dark street at night, and all your senses are switched on? You are hyperaware of every sound and every flicker of light. Your body is on high alert, and your brain's fear centre is switched on even if you don't need it.
- This quick response was crucial for survival in dangerous environments. On many occasions, the reaction time was the difference between whether you survived or not.
- Our brains are biased towards negative information (negativity bias) as a protective mechanism. We can actively change this negative information by re-framing the situation, what we think and, more often than not, the outcome.

Misfiring in modern contexts:

- While helpful for immediate physical dangers, this amygdala switching itself on a system isn't always suited for modern stressors. These days we don't have lions to run from or wild creatures hunting us as prey. But we have situations such as work deadlines, tasks that must be carried out, stressful relationships, bills, debts etc.
- Chronic activation of the stress response in non-life-threatening situations can lead to anxiety disorders such as withdrawals, heart palpitations, agitation and constant worry.
- Modern life presents many abstract threats (like job insecurity) that can trigger the same anxiety response as physical dangers.

- Understanding the evolutionary basis of anxiety can help in re-framing anxious thoughts, helping to manage stress and allowing you to develop coping strategies. Remember, your anxiety is an ancient survival tool trying its best to protect you in a modern world it wasn't designed for.

REFLECTING ON YOUR PROGRESS:

As we conclude this chapter, please take a moment to congratulate yourself and acknowledge the steps you've taken to understand anxiety. Remember, awareness is the first step towards effective management.

Interactive Element: Chapter Achievements

1. What is the one new insight you have gained about anxiety?

2. Has your understanding of your anxiety changed?

3. How do you think your understanding of your anxiety has changed?

4. What is one small win that you can celebrate in terms of recognizing your anxiety patterns?

UNDERSTANDING ANXIETY

Chapter 1 Summary:

Congratulations! You've just completed an in-depth look at anxiety and its many facets. You will now understand what anxiety is, how it manifests in your life's situations, and why it exists. Always remember that "knowledge is power." understanding your anxiety, its effects, and its cause is the first step towards being able to manage it effectively.

In the next chapter, we'll dive into the fascinating world of the anxious brain, exploring how your mind and body work together in moments of anxiety.

Get ready to become your own personal neuroscientist!"

CHAPTER 2
THE ANXIOUS BRAIN

Welcome to your very own personal neuroscience crash course!

Don't get stressed or start worrying, we won't be performing any brain surgery today just doing some fascinating exploration of "the anxious mind."

Understanding how anxiety affects your brain can help you feel more in control of your experiences. Let's do a little exploring into the key players in your brain's anxiety response:

THE NEUROSCIENCE OF ANXIETY

Imagine your brain as a bustling city. There are many different neighbourhoods; let's call these the "brain regions" These neighbourhoods communicate with each other, but they communicate via an intricate subway system called the neural pathways. (no mobile phones, not even a fax machine in sight). In an anxious brain, some trains run too fast, while others might be delayed.

. . .

THE ANXIOUS BRAIN

Key brain regions involved in anxiety:

Amygdala: The city's alarm system

- Function: To process emotions, particularly the "fight or flight" response.
- In anxiety: Becomes overactive, setting off false alarms, causing anxiety levels to rise and persist.

Hippocampus: The city's historian

- Function: Involved in memory formation, emotional feelings, and how you see things.
- In anxiety: The Hippocampus may shrink due to chronic stress, affecting both memory and mood regulation.

Prefrontal Cortex: The city's planning department

- Function: Regulates emotions and behaviours, allowing you to choose how you respond and behave.
- In anxiety: Struggles to calm the overactive amygdala, keeping your body and your senses on high alert, keeps your anxiety levels high.

Anterior Cingulate Cortex: The city's conflict resolution centre

- Function: Helps in decision-making and emotional regulation
- In anxiety: May show altered activity, leading to difficulty in managing the level of worry.

NEUROTRANSMITTERS AND ANXIETY

Now if you think of neurotransmitters as the brain's text message service, in anxiety, some of these messages get garbled or sent too frequently."

Key neurotransmitters:

Serotonin: The "feel-good" messenger

- Standard function: Regulates your mood, your sleep, and your appetite.
- In anxiety: Levels may be low, contributing to anxious feelings.
- **GABA (Gamma-Amino-butyric Acid)**: The "chill out" messenger
- Standard function: Reduces neuron excitability
- In anxiety: May be underactive, leading to heightened arousal and exaggerated emotions.

Norepinephrine: The "alertness" messenger

- Standard function: Increases alertness and arousal.
- In anxiety: Can be overactive, contributing to feelings of panic, fear and anxiety.

Did You Know? Many anti-anxiety medications work by altering the levels or effects of these neurotransmitters on the body.

THE FIGHT, FLIGHT, OR FREEZE RESPONSE

Your body's alarm system hasn't had any significant kind of upgrade since our cave-dwelling days. It's like using a flip phone in the age of smartphones, or worse, smoke signals instead of computers. Things and times have moved on and changed, but the body's response to "Fight or flight" has stayed the same.

Trigger: A perceived threat activates the amygdala

Autonomic Nervous System Activation:

- The sympathetic branch ("fight or flight") jumps up and starts letting you know it's there.
- The parasympathetic branch ("rest and digest") dials down.

Physical Changes:

- Increased heart rate and breathing
- Dilated pupils
- Blood flow is redirected to major muscle groups and away from others.
- Digestion slows as the body redirects energy and blood flow.
- Sweat production increases

Myth: The fight, flight or freeze response is always harmful to your body.

Fact: This response can be life-saving in hazardous situations. It's only problematic when activated too frequently or intensely in non-threatening situations.

HOW ANXIETY AFFECTS YOUR THINKING

Anxiety can turn your mind into a fun house mirror; it can distort your thoughts and perceptions, throw you into confusion and make you question what it is you are seeing and what you are feeling, and sometimes even the reality of the situation.

Cognitive effects of anxiety:

- **Attentional Bias**: Becoming hyper-focused on potential threats, e.g. In a room full of smiling people, you only notice the one frowning face.
- **Catastrophist**: Jumping to worst-case scenarios: e.g., a headache must be a brain tumour; a delayed text response means the person hates you or isn't interested.
- **Overgeneralization**: Applying one negative experience to all similar situations, e.g. Jumbling words during one presentation, means you will need to improve at all public speaking events.

- **Mind-Reading**: Assuming you know what others are thinking, usually negatively e.g. Believing your co-workers think you're incompetent without any evidence or proof, only what you are thinking in your mind.

HOW ANXIETY AFFECTS BEHAVIOUR:

Anxiety isn't just an internal experience, it can significantly shape how we think, act, react and behave in the world.

Common anxiety-driven behaviours:

Avoidance: Steering clear of anxiety-triggering situations:

Pros: Provides short-term relief

Con: Reinforces anxiety in the long term

- **Safety Behaviours:** Actions taken to prevent feared outcomes, e.g. Over-preparing for every possible question before a social event. Consequence: Prevents learning that fears are often unfounded and is usually an over-exaggeration of the mind and worry.
- **Reassurance Seeking:** Constantly ask others for assurance, e.g., repeatedly asking a partner if they still love you. Consequence: Provides temporary relief but can strain your relationships.
- **Procrastination:** Putting off tasks due to performance anxiety, e.g., Delaying starting a project due to fear of failure. Consequence: Increases stress and often confirms anxious beliefs.

Journal Prompt: This is a time when you can take out your journal and begin writing. Reflect on your behaviours. Can you identify and write down any of your behaviours that might be driven by anxiety?"

THE ANXIETY-SLEEP CONNECTION

Anxiety and poor sleep are like troublesome twins where one goes, the other often follows.

How anxiety disrupts sleep:

- Racing thoughts make it hard to relax and fall asleep.
- Waking from sleep due to anxious dreams or thoughts going around in your head.
- Difficulty returning to sleep after waking up.

How poor sleep exacerbates anxiety:

- Sleep deprivation can increase activity in the amygdala.
- Lack of sleep impairs the prefrontal cortex's ability to regulate emotions.
- Fatigue can be misinterpreted as a sign of anxiety, creating a vicious cycle.

Studies show that improving your sleep quality can significantly reduce anxiety symptoms.

THE ROLE OF GENETICS:

Your genes aren't your destiny, but they can stack the deck when it comes to anxiety.

- Specific genes linked to anxiety include those involved in the neurotransmitter systems and stress responses.
- Epigenetics: Environmental factors can influence how genes are expressed, potentially "turning on" or "off" anxiety-related genes.

Remember: Having a genetic predisposition doesn't guarantee you'll develop an anxiety disorder. Environmental factors and personal experiences play a crucial role.

REFLECTING ON YOUR PROGRESS:

As we conclude this chapter, take a moment to acknowledge your growing understanding of the neuroscience behind anxiety. You are doing very well. Step by step, we will take you there.

Interactive Element: Chapter Achievements

1. What is one key fact you learned about how anxiety affects the brain?

| |
| |

2. How could this knowledge help you when managing your anxiety?

| |
| |

3. What is the one small win you can celebrate regarding understanding your body's anxiety response?

| |
| |

Fantastic, another chapter is complete, you are gaining valuable insights into the workings of your anxious brain.

Chapter 2 Summary:

Congratulations! You've just completed a whirlwind tour of your anxious brain. You are now able to come to grips with the knowledge that underpins the biological factors of anxiety as a crucial step in learning how to manage anxiety.

In the next chapter, we'll explore how to identify your anxiety triggers.

CHAPTER 3

IDENTIFYING YOUR ANXIETY TRIGGERS:

In this chapter, we'll equip you with the tools to uncover the culprits behind your anxiety. Remember, "knowledge is power", and understanding your triggers is the first step to mastering them."

WHAT ARE ANXIETY TRIGGERS?

Imagine that your anxiety is a sleeping dragon. The triggers are the alarm clocks that wake up the dragon."

Definition: Anxiety triggers are specific situations, places, objects, or experiences that bring on your feelings of anxiety and your anxiety symptoms.

Importance: Understanding what your triggers are will help you:

- Predict and prepare for anxious moments so you can decide how to manage the feelings and the situation.
- Develop, practised and targeted coping strategies
- Gain a sense of control over your anxiety.

IDENTIFYING YOUR ANXIETY TRIGGERS:

Did You Know? Triggers can be both external (like public speaking) and internal (like specific thoughts, usually negative, that are on your mind or physical sensations).

COMMON ANXIETY TRIGGERS:

While each person's anxiety is specific and unique, there are some usual suspects in the lineup of triggers.

External Anxiety Triggers:

- Social situations.
- Work or school pressures.
- Financial stress.
- Health concerns.
- Major life changes.
- Conflict in relationships.
- Crowded or confined spaces.
- Specific phobias (heights, spiders, cats, etc.)

Internal Anxiety Triggers:

- Negative self-talk
- Perfectionism (feeling that you or situations aren't going right or you could do it better)
- Uncertainty or lack of control over yourself or a situation.
- Physical sensations (rapid heartbeat, dizziness, feeling overwhelmed, sweating)
- Traumatic memories
- Lack of sleep or poor nutrition

Interactive Element 1: "Trigger Tracker" Checklist of common triggers.

Instructions:

1. Review the list of common triggers below.
2. Check the boxes next to triggers that resonate with you.
3. Add any personal triggers not listed in the space provided.

External Triggers:

☐ Social situations

☐ Work or school pressures

☐ Financial stress

☐ Health concerns

☐ Major life changes

☐ Conflict in relationships

☐ Crowded or confined spaces

☐ Specific phobias (heights, spiders, etc.)

Internal Triggers:

☐ Negative self-talk

☐ Perfectionism

☐ Uncertainty or lack of control

☐ Physical sensations (rapid heartbeat, dizziness)

☐ Traumatic memories

☐ Lack of sleep or poor nutrition

IDENTIFYING YOUR ANXIETY TRIGGERS:

```
[                                                    ]
```

Your personal triggers:

```
[                                                    ]

[                                                    ]

[                                                    ]
```

THE ANXIETY JOURNAL:

Think of your anxiety journal as your personal detective's notebook. This is where you'll gather clues and solve the mystery of your anxiety. You will be writing down how you are feeling, the circumstances, what is happening or even the outcome, you will get a clearer understanding of your particular anxiety issues and how they affect you. This is a step in the right direction of being able to manage your anxiety effectively.

How to keep an anxiety journal: (write the following points down in your journal.)

- Date and time of the anxious episode.
- Situation or event preceding anxiety.
- Thoughts and emotions experienced (try to recall what you were thinking?)
- Physical symptoms (what changes were in your body, breathing etc.?)
- Intensity of anxiety (scale of 1-10).
- Coping methods used and their effectiveness.

Myth: Journaling about anxiety will make you more anxious.

Fact: While it may feel uncomfortable at first, journaling can help you gain insight, perspective and control over your anxiety in the long run.

Interactive Element 2: Anxiety Journal Template

Instructions: Use this template to record your next anxious experience.

Date and time: _____

Situation or event preceding anxiety:

| |
| |

Thoughts experienced:

| |
| |

Emotions felt:

| |
| |

Physical symptoms that you felt at the time:

| |
| |

Intensity of anxiety (on a scale of 1 – 10) ____

. . .

IDENTIFYING YOUR ANXIETY TRIGGERS:

A coping strategy that was used:

Effectiveness of coping strategy:

Journal prompt: Start your anxiety journal today. Record the next anxious experience you have using the format above.

RECOGNIZING THOUGHT PATTERNS:

Our thoughts are like invisible strings pulling the puppet of our emotions. Let's learn to see those strings and try to control how they work and what each string does.

Common anxious thought patterns:

- **Catastrophist**: "If I fail this exam, my whole career is over."
- **Overgeneralization** Overgeneralization: "I felt anxious at the last party. I'll never enjoy social events."
- **Mind reading:** "Everyone at this gathering thinks I'm boring, and I am sure they are laughing at me."
- **Should statements:** "I should be able to handle this without feeling anxious."
- **Emotional reasoning**: "I feel scared, so this situation must be dangerous, and I don't want to be in a dangerous place."

Interactive Element 3: Thought Pattern Detective

Instructions: Read each scenario and identify the type of anxious thought pattern at play. Choose from Catastrophist, Overgeneralization, Mind reading, Should statements and Emotional reasoning.

Scenario 1: "If I make a mistake in this presentation, my whole career is over.

Thought pattern:

Scenario 2: "I felt anxious at the last party. I'll never enjoy social events."

Thought pattern:

Scenario 3: "Everyone at this gathering thinks I'm boring.

Thought pattern:

Scenario 4: "I should be able to handle this without feeling anxious.

Thought pattern:

IDENTIFYING YOUR ANXIETY TRIGGERS:

```
┌─────────────────────────────────────────────┐
│                                             │
│                                             │
│                                             │
└─────────────────────────────────────────────┘
```

Scenario 5: I feel scared, so this situation must be dangerous.

Thought pattern:

```
┌─────────────────────────────────────────────┐
│                                             │
│                                             │
│                                             │
└─────────────────────────────────────────────┘
```

THE ROLE OF AVOIDANCE:

Avoidance is anxiety's best friend. It might feel helpful in the moment, but it's secretly making your anxiety stronger. It is stopping you from getting things done.

How avoidance reinforces anxiety:

- Short-term relief vs. long-term consequences
- The anxiety paradox: The more you avoid, the more anxious you become
- Missed opportunities for building confidence and coping skills

Example: Sarah avoids all social gatherings due to social anxiety. While this reduces her immediate anxiety, it reinforces her belief that social situations are threatening, and this thought prevents her from learning that she can handle them.

1. Uncovering Hidden Triggers:

Sometimes anxiety triggers are like ninjas, stealthy, hidden and hard to spot. Let's shine a light on these hidden culprits and bring them out into the open.

Techniques for identifying hidden triggers:

- Mindfulness practices to increase your self-awareness.
- Tracking anxiety patterns and how you are feeling in your anxiety journal.
- Discuss your situation with a trusted friend or a therapist.
- Considering or thinking about past experiences and trauma.

Did You Know? Sometimes, positive events can trigger anxiety. This is known as "positive anxiety" or "eustress."

1. The Trigger-Response-Consequence Model:

Understanding how the full cycle of your anxiety works can help you intervene at any point.

Breakdown of the model:

- **Trigger**: The event or thought that begins the feelings and symptoms of anxiety.
- **Response**: Your immediate reaction (thoughts, feelings, behaviours)
- **Consequence**: The outcome of your response (what did you do? How did you cope?)

Example:

- **Trigger**: Receiving a vague "We need to talk" text from your boss or partner.
- **Response**: Catastrophic thoughts, increased heart rate, difficulty focusing or concentrating on work
- **Consequence**: You spent the day distracted and anxious, which affected my work performance. You feel anxious and have no outcome.

Interactive Element: "Map Your Anxiety" Create your own Trigger-Response-Consequence map for a recent anxious experience.

IDENTIFYING YOUR ANXIETY TRIGGERS:

Interactive Element 4: Map Your Anxiety

Instructions: Review a recent anxious experience and fill out this Trigger-Response-Consequence map.

Trigger:

Response:

Thoughts:

Feelings:

Behaviours:

Consequence:

CREATING A TRIGGER HIERARCHY:

Not all anxiety triggers are created equal. Let's organize them from 'slightly unsettling' to 'full-blown panic.

Steps to creating a trigger hierarchy:

1. List all of the anxiety triggers that you have identified.
2. Rate each trigger on a scale of 0-100 for anxiety intensity.
3. Arrange triggers from lowest to highest intensity.

Benefits of a trigger hierarchy:

- Provides a roadmap for introducing and going through gradual exposure therapy.
- It will help prioritize the most important triggers, which should be addressed first.
- Gives a sense of being in control and a level of organization to your anxiety management.

Interactive Element 5: Create Your Trigger Hierarchy

Instructions: List your anxiety triggers and rate each on a scale of 0-100 for anxiety intensity. Then, rewrite them in order from lowest to highest intensity.

Trigger: Intensity (0-100)

1		0-100	
2		0-100	
3		0-100	
4		0-100	
5		0-100	

IDENTIFYING YOUR ANXIETY TRIGGERS:

Reordered intensity from lowest to highest:

1	
2	
3	
4	
5	

REFLECTING ON YOUR PROGRESS:

As we conclude this chapter, take a moment to acknowledge the work you've done in identifying your anxiety triggers.

Interactive Element 6: Chapter Achievements

1. What is the most important trigger that you have become aware of?

2. How will recognizing this trigger help you to manage your anxiety more effectively?

3. In terms of understanding your anxiety patterns, what is one small win you can celebrate?

Congratulations! This chapter is now complete. You have gained important insights about your anxiety.

Chapter 3 Summary:

Excellent, give yourself a pat on the back; you have just become a real inspector, Clouseau and an expert anxiety detector. From now on, you will be armed with your new knowledge of thought patterns, triggers and the anxiety cycle. You are well-equipped to understand more about your anxiety, and this will allow you to start taking control and managing your stress. The next chapter is coming up and in this chapter, we will explore important and powerful techniques for re-framing and challenging the anxious thoughts you have identified.

CHAPTER 4
CHALLENGING ANXIOUS THOUGHTS:

Let me welcome you to your workout plan. In this chapter, you will be working hard as you flex your mental muscles and push yourself to challenge and reshape the annoying anxiety thoughts. You can do this, remember you are much stronger than your anxiety will allow you to believe.

UNDERSTANDING COGNITIVE DISTORTIONS:

Do you remember going to the fair and into the fun house? Yes, the room with all the mirrors? It made you feel as if you didn't know which mirror to look at, and all the reflections looking back at you seemed unreal and distorted in so many ways. This may be a strange comparison, but cognitive distortions are like funhouse mirrors for your mind; they distort reality in ways that fuel anxiety.

Common cognitive distortions:

- **All-or-nothing thinking**: Seeing things in black-and-white categories gives no room for another way of thinking or no room to be swayed or convinced otherwise.

- **Overgeneralization**: Viewing a single negative event as a never-ending pattern of defeat and worrying that the one event is set to be a long-term pattern and outcome of each event.
- **Mental Filter**: Focus solely on the negative details, ignore the positives of the situation, and have a skewed and one-sided view (negative) of things.
- **Jumping to Conclusions**: Making negative interpretations without supporting facts. Taking an opposing viewpoint without any evidence or confirmation.
- **Magnification (Catastrophist) or Minimization**: Exaggerating the importance of problems. Making the problem seem much larger than it is, minimizing and downplaying your positive qualities, and also feeling that your input is of little or no importance.
- **Emotional Reasoning**: Assuming that negative emotions reflect reality when you are not looking at the whole picture or the bigger picture and feeling that how you feel must be accurate and not looking at what has happened or the facts of the situation.
- **Should Statements:** Criticizing yourself or others with "shoulds" and "musts", placing blame when unhappy about an outcome.
- **Labelling**: Attaching a negative label to yourself or others instead of describing the specific behaviour.
- **Personalization**: Seeing yourself as the cause of some negative external event for which you weren't primarily responsible.

CHALLENGING ANXIOUS THOUGHTS:

Interactive Element 1: Distortion Detective

Instructions: Match each statement with the cognitive distortion it represents.

Statements:

1. "I made a mistake on this report. I'm a total failure."
2. "She didn't smile at me. She must hate me."
3. "I should always be productive."
4. "I feel anxious, so this situation must be dangerous."
5. "Nothing ever goes right for me."

Cognitive Distortions:

A. Overgeneralization
B. Jumping to conclusions
C. Should statements
D. Emotional reasoning
E. All-or-Nothing thinking

(Answers 1=E, 2=B, 3=C, 4=D, 5=A)

THE POWER OF THOUGHT RECORDS:

Thought records are like instant replay for your mind. They allow you to pause, rewind, and objectively examine your thoughts. Often we don't take the time to look back at events and situations that upset us, unless we are thinking what should have or could have been said or done. Thought records give you that opportunity.

Steps to create a thought record:

1. **Situation:** Describe the event or situation that led to the unpleasant emotion.
2. **Emotion:** Take the time to identify your emotion and then rate the intensity of your emotion.

3. **Automatic Thought:** Write down the initial thought that accompanied the emotion.
4. **Evidence That Supports The Thought:** List the facts that support your thought as best you can.
5. **Evidence That Doesn't Support The Thought**: Think about and list the facts that contradict your thought.
6. **Alternative Thought:** Generate a more balanced thought based on all the evidence. You can take this opportunity to be creative with your thinking here.
7. **Re-rate Emotion**: After coming up with an alternative thought, rate your emotion's intensity.

Interactive Element 2: Thought Record Practice

Instructions: Use a recent event/situation where you experienced being anxious to fill out the thought record below:

Situation:

Emotion and Intensity (0-100):

Automatic Thought:

CHALLENGING ANXIOUS THOUGHTS:

Evidence For:

| |
| |

Evidence Against:

| |
| |

Alternative Thought:

| |
| |

New Emotion Intensity (0-100): _____

SOCRATIC QUESTIONING:

Named after Socrates, Socratic questioning is a method of education that primarily focuses on getting answers by asking students questions. It was thought that the practice of thoughtful questioning allowed the student to challenge assumptions, examine, analyse and look at complicated ideas to find out the truth or validity of those ideas. The teacher will characterize an ignorant mindset and force the student to get to a higher knowledge level, whilst acknowledging contradictions they will recreate an idea and use appropriate thinking to finish the idea and with a critical view to determine what thought was needed to get to a conclusion. Students were encouraged to look at what is known from what is not known, follow a logical course of thinking and think about their answer or response.

· Socratic questioning helps you examine your thoughts more critically.

· Socratic questioning is a technique that involves asking yourself probing questions to challenge anxious thoughts, explore different perspectives, and uncover more balanced, realistic views. It's like having a thoughtful conversation with yourself to examine your assumptions more critically.

Key Socratic questions:

- What evidence do I have to support this thought?
- Is there an alternative explanation?
- What's the worst thing that could happen?
- How likely is it that the worst-case scenario could happen?
- What is the best that could happen?
- What is the thing that is most likely to happen?
- What would I tell a friend in this situation?

Interactive Element 3: Socratic Dialogue

Instructions: Use Socratic questioning to challenge the following anxious thoughts:

"I'll mess up my presentation and everyone will think I'm incompetent."

1. What evidence do I have that supports this thought?

CHALLENGING ANXIOUS THOUGHTS:

2. Is there an alternative explanation?

3. What is the worst that could happen?

4. How likely is it that the worst-case scenario could happen?

5. What is the best that could happen?

6. What is the thing that is most likely to happen?

7. What would I tell a friend in this situation?

8. Cognitive Restructuring: (Use this line to write down a thought you can replace with a more balanced and realistic thought.)

Think of cognitive restructuring as home renovation for your mind. You are not moving out, we're not tearing everything down, just remodelling certain parts to make it work better for you.

Steps in cognitive restructuring:

1. Identify the negative thought.
2. Challenge the thought using evidence and logic.
3. Replace that thought with a more balanced, thought out and realistic thought.

Example:

1. Negative thought: "I always mess up in social situations."
2. Challenge: Is it always? Can you think of times when you have succeeded or felt good in a social situation?
3. Balanced thought: "While I sometimes feel awkward, I've had many positive social interactions too."

MINDFULNESS AND ACCEPTANCE:

Sometimes the best way to deal with anxious thoughts is to not fight them but observe them without judgment.

Mindfulness techniques:

- **Thought labelling:** Do nothing but note the "thinking" when you notice a thought.
- **Leaves on a stream:** Imagine placing each thought on a leaf and watching it float away

CHALLENGING ANXIOUS THOUGHTS:

- **Thanking your mind:** Acknowledge the thought by saying "Thanks, mind" and letting it go.

Interactive Element 4: Mindful Moment

Instructions: You can use a clock or your phone for this,

- Set a timer for 2 minutes.
- Close your eyes and focus on your breath.
- Each time a thought arises, label it "thinking" and return to your breath.
- After the exercise, note how often you noticed and labelled a thought.
- Number of thoughts labelled: _____

1. Exposure Techniques:

Having the courage to face your fears head-on can be a powerful way to challenge anxious thoughts and give you the confidence to deal with situations effectively.

Types of exposure:

- **In vivo:** (living organism/human testing) Real-life exposure to feared situations
- Imaginal: Visualizing feared scenarios by seeing the images in your mind.
- Interoception: By inducing feared physical sensations so that they can be identified and named. (hunger is such a feeling)

Steps for creating an exposure hierarchy:

1. List anxiety-provoking situations
2. Rate each situation from 0-100 based on anxiety level
3. Arrange situations from the least anxiety-provoking to the most anxiety-provoking.

4. Start with the least anxiety-provoking and work your way upwards.

Interactive Element 5: My Exposure Hierarchy

Instructions: Create a simple exposure hierarchy for a specific fear.

Fear: _____

Situations:

1		Anxiety Level 0-100
2		Anxiety Level 0-100
3		Anxiety Level 0-100
4		Anxiety Level 0-100
5		Anxiety Level 0-100

Put your anxious thoughts to the test with real-world experiments.

Steps for a behavioural experiment:

1. Identify the anxious prediction.
2. Design an experiment to test the prediction.
3. Carry out the experiment.
4. Evaluate the results.
5. Draw conclusions.

Example: Prediction: "If I speak up in a meeting, everyone will think I'm stupid."

Experiment: Contribute one idea in the next team meeting

Result: Colleagues responded positively to the idea

Conclusion: Speaking up doesn't always lead to negative outcomes

CHALLENGING ANXIOUS THOUGHTS:

Interactive Element 6: Design Your Experiment

Instructions: Design a simple behavioural experiment to test one of your anxious thoughts.

Anxious thought:

Experiment design:

Predicted outcome:

Actual outcome:

Conclusion:

REFLECTING ON YOUR PROGRESS:

As we end this chapter, please take a moment to acknowledge the skills you've learned and developed in challenging anxious thoughts. Take a little time to reflect and congratulate yourself.

Interactive Element: Chapter Achievements

1. Write down one of the cognitive distortions you have learned to recognize.

2. Write down one of the ways you have applied or plan to apply thought-challenging techniques.

3. Regarding changing your thought patterns, what one small win can you celebrate?

Congratulations on completing this chapter. You are doing well and developing powerful tools to help you manage and reshape your thinking!

Chapter Summary:

You've just added a robust set of tools to your anxiety-busting toolkit. Remember, challenging anxious thoughts is a skill that improves with practice. In the next chapter, we'll explore how mindfulness can

CHALLENGING ANXIOUS THOUGHTS:

further enhance your ability to manage anxiety and boost your confidence.

CHAPTER 5
UNDERSTANDING AND MANAGING PANIC ATTACKS

WHAT IS A PANIC ATTACK?

A panic attack is a sudden surge of overwhelming anxiety and fear. It typically reaches its peak within minutes and can include a range of physical symptoms such as:

- Rapid heartbeat or palpitations
- Sweating
- Trembling or shaking
- Shortness of breath
- Chest pain or discomfort
- Nausea
- Problems with vision
- Feelings of detachment
- Fear of losing control or "going crazy"
- Fear of dying
- Stomach problems
- Dizziness or light-headedness
- Becoming disoriented

UNDERSTANDING AND MANAGING PANIC ATTACKS

It is essential for you to realize and understand that while panic attacks can be extremely frightening, They are not physically dangerous, and most symptoms fade away once the panic attack dissipates.

THE PHYSIOLOGY OF PANIC ATTACKS

During a panic attack, your body's fight-or-flight response goes into overdrive. The response which was ultimately designed to protect you from danger, now causes a surge of adrenaline that leads to the physical symptoms you can experience. While you are not in any real danger, the feeling of being in the middle of a panic attack and out of control can be very frightening and worrying.

Vital physiological changes include:

- Increased heart rate and blood pressure
- Rapid breathing (hyperventilation)
- Blood flow is redirected to major muscle groups
- Digestion slows down
- Heightened senses

Interactive Element: Body Map of Panic

On the outline of a human body below, mark where you typically feel sensations during a panic attack. Write brief descriptions of how these sensations feel.

[Insert simple body outline diagram]

COMMON TRIGGERS FOR PANIC ATTACKS:

Panic attacks can be triggered by specific situations, or they may seem to come "out of the blue". Common triggers can include such things as:

- Stressful life events
- Specific environments (e.g., crowded places, being in front of an audience, enclosed spaces)

- Physical sensations (e.g., increased heart rate, sweating, clammy hands)
- Intense emotions of fear, being out of control, or even wanting to run away.
- Specific thought patterns of negativity or fear can bring on the panic attack and can sometimes stay until well after other symptoms have calmed down or gone altogether.

Interactive Element: Identifying My Triggers

List potential triggers for your panic attacks:

THE PANIC CYCLE

The panic cycle illustrates how panic attacks can perpetuate themselves:

1. Trigger (internal or external)
2. Perceived threat
3. Anxiety and physical sensations
4. Catastrophic misinterpretation of sensations
5. Increased anxiety and more intense physical sensations

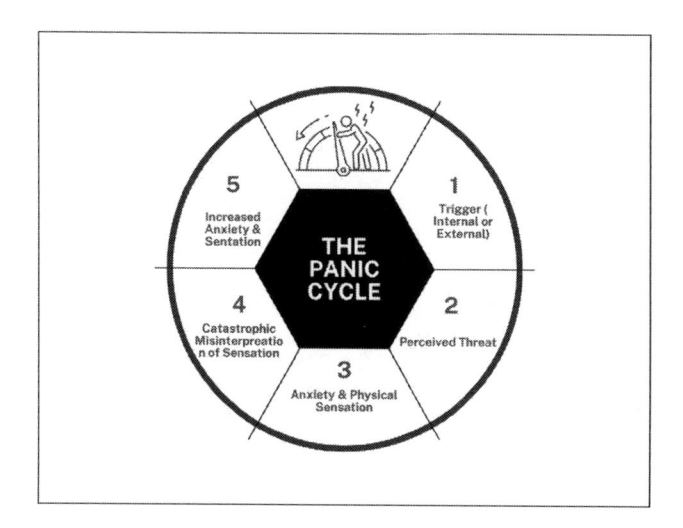

THE PANIC CYCLE

1. Trigger (Internal or External)
2. Perceived Threat
3. Anxiety & Physical Sensation
4. Catastrophic Misinterpreation of Sensation
5. Increased Anxiety & Sentation

Understanding what is happening and being able to break the cycle and control the intense sensations are key to managing panic attacks.

Interactive Element: My Panic Attack Profile

Record details of your panic attacks so that you will be able to identify recurring patterns:

Day	Time	Trigger	Symptoms	Duration	Strategy Used / Effectiveness (1 - 10)
Mon					
Tue					
Wed					
Thu					
Fri					
Sat					
Sun					

STRATEGIES FOR MANAGING PANIC ATTACKS:

Breathing Techniques

a) **Diaphragmatic Breathing:**

- Place one hand on your chest and the other on your belly
- Breathe in slowly through your nose, feeling your belly expand
- Exhale slowly through your mouth
- Repeat using 5-10 breaths

b) **4-7-8 Breathing:**

- Inhale quietly through your nose for 4 seconds
- Hold your breath for 7 seconds
- Exhale completely through your mouth for 8 seconds
- Repeat this exercise for four cycles

1. ***Grounding Exercises:***

a) 5-4-3-2-1 Technique: Identify:

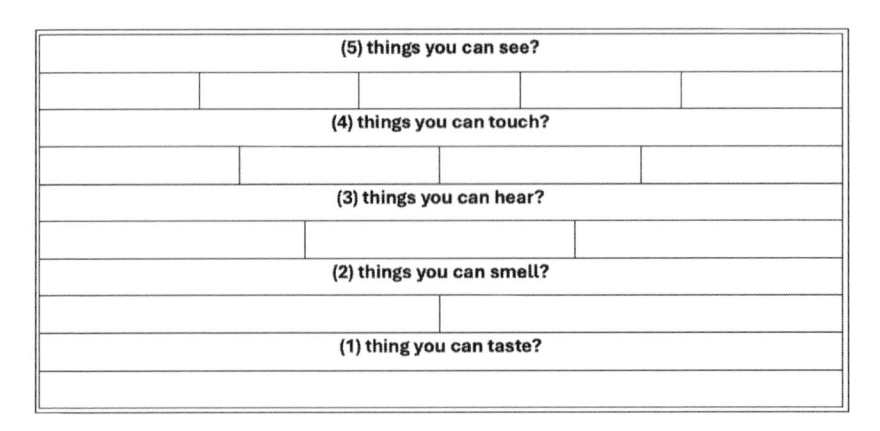

(5) things you can see?						
(4) things you can touch?						
(3) things you can hear?						
(2) things you can smell?						
(1) thing you can taste?						

b) Object focus: Choose an object in your environment and describe it in detail (colour, texture, shape, scent, etc.)

UNDERSTANDING AND MANAGING PANIC ATTACKS

```
┌─────────────────────────────────────────┐
│                                         │
│                                         │
│                                         │
│                                         │
└─────────────────────────────────────────┘
```

Cognitive Strategies

a) Reality Testing: Ask yourself:

What is the evidence that supports my fear?

```
┌─────────────────────────────────────────┐
└─────────────────────────────────────────┘
```

What's the evidence against my fear?

```
┌─────────────────────────────────────────┐
└─────────────────────────────────────────┘
```

What's the most likely outcome?

```
┌─────────────────────────────────────────┐
└─────────────────────────────────────────┘
```

b) Positive Self-Talk: Develop calming phrases like:

- "This will pass."
- "I am safe."
- "I've been through this before and come through it, I know I can do it again."

Gradual Exposure:

Creating a fear hierarchy and gradually exposing yourself to feared situations can help reduce panic over time.

. . .

Interactive Element: My Panic Attack Toolkit

List your go-to strategies for effectively managing your panic attacks:

Breathing Techniques	
Grounding Exercises	
Cognitive Strategy	
Positive Self-Talk phrase	
Other	

PREVENTING PANIC ATTACKS:

While it's not always possible to prevent panic attacks entirely, knowing these strategies and practising them can help reduce the frequency of panic attacks and their intensity:

1. **Regular Exercise**: Aim for at least 30 minutes of moderate exercise most days of the week.

2. **Adequate Sleep**: Establish a consistent sleep schedule and practice good sleep hygiene.

3. **Balanced Die**t: Avoid excessive caffeine and alcohol, eat regular meals, and stay hydrated.

4. **Stress Management:** Practice relaxation techniques like progressive muscle relaxation or meditation daily.

5. **Mindfulness**: Regular mindfulness practice can help you stay grounded in the present moment.

UNDERSTANDING AND MANAGING PANIC ATTACKS

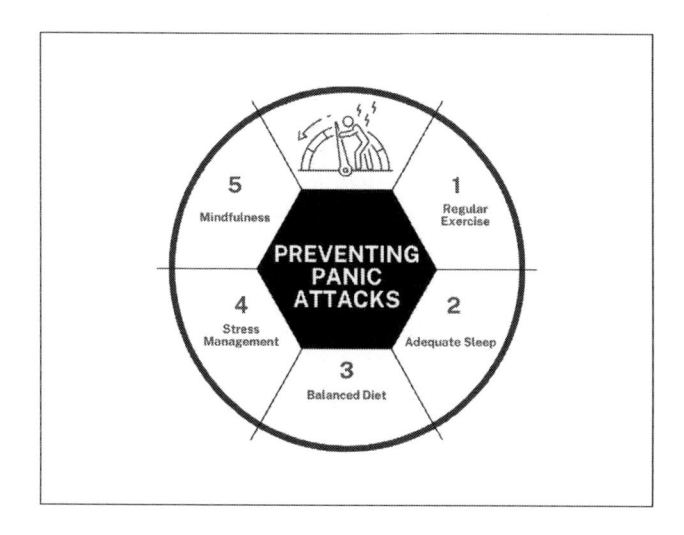

Preventing Panic Attacks diagram: 1. Regular Exercise, 2. Adequate Sleep, 3. Balanced Diet, 4. Stress Management, 5. Mindfulness

Interactive Element: My Prevention Plan

Create a plan for your daily life that also incorporates panic attack prevention strategies.

1. Sleep schedule:

[   ]

2. Dietary changes:

[   ]

3. Daily relaxation practice:

[   ]

4. Mindfulness technique:

[   ]

WHEN TO SEEK PROFESSIONAL HELP

Consider seeking professional help if:

- Panic attacks are frequent or severe.
- You find yourself avoiding certain situations due to the fear of panic attacks.
- Panic attacks are significantly impacting your quality of life.

Effective treatments for panic disorder include:

- Cognitive Behavioural Therapy (CBT)
- Exposure Therapy
- Medication (in some cases)

REFLECTING ON YOUR PROGRESS

As we come to the end of this chapter, I want you to take a moment to acknowledge your growing understanding of what a panic attack is and how to manage a panic attack in the future.

Interactive Element: Chapter Achievements

Write down one new strategy you have learned to help manage panic attacks.

```
┌─────────────────────────────────────┐
│                                     │
│                                     │
└─────────────────────────────────────┘
```

How has your point of view on panic attacks changed?

```
┌─────────────────────────────────────┐
│                                     │
│                                     │
└─────────────────────────────────────┘
```

In terms of getting ready for panic attacks and facing them, what is one small win that you can celebrate?

>

Congratulations on reaching this chapter's end and gaining valuable insights and the tools to handle future panic attacks!

Chapter Summary:

Panic attacks, while worrying and intensely frightening, are manageable with the right tools and strategies. When you can understand the physiology of panic, identify your triggers, and practise coping techniques and strategies, you can significantly reduce the impact that panic attacks can have on your life. Be gentle with yourself, and remember that it is a process that takes time and patience. The next chapter will explore how mindfulness can further support your anxiety management journey.

CHAPTER 6
MINDFULNESS AND ANXIETY

We are moving on in this chapter and will explore how mindfulness can help you and be your own secret weapon against anxiety. You are now ready to train your mind to be on your side, not your enemy.

INTRODUCTION TO MINDFULNESS

Mindfulness is focusing your mind and your attention on what is happening now, in the moment and being physically, emotionally and mentally present without any expectations or judgement.

Mindfulness is similar to a gym workout for your mind. With regular practice, your mental muscles will become much stronger.

Key principles of mindfulness:

- Being aware and present in the moment.
- Observation with no preconceived ideas or judgment.
- Accept and acknowledge your thoughts and how you are feeling.

- Have a curious and open mind, allowing for new ideas and concepts.

Benefits for anxiety:

- Reduces rumination.
- Enhances emotional regulation.
- Improves your stress response.
- Increases self-awareness.

Research has shown that practising mindfulness regularly can change the structure of your brain, especially the areas involved in memory, emotional regulation, learning motion regulation, and understanding new ideas and concepts.

THE SCIENCE BEHIND MINDFULNESS

We will look more closely to see how mindfulness works on your anxious brain.

Neurological effects of mindfulness:

- Reduces activity in the brain's alarm system (the amygdala)
- Increases activity in the area involved in rational thinking (prefrontal cortex)
- The act of mindfulness strengthens the connection between the amygdala and the prefrontal cortex
- Increases Gray matter density in areas related to learning, memory, and emotional regulation.

Physiological effects:

- Lowers blood pressure and heart rate.
- Reduced levels of the stress hormone cortisol.
- Improves your immune function.

Interactive Element 1: Brain Benefits Bingo

Instructions: As you go through this chapter and practice mindfulness, mark off the benefits you experience.

☐ Feeling calmer

☐ Less reactive to stressful situations

☐ Improved level of focus

☐ Better sleep

☐ Reduced muscle tension

☐ Thinking with more clarity

☐ An increased level of self-awareness

☐ More patience

☐ Improved mood

Mindfulness Exercises for Anxiety

Like any skill, you need practice to improve; with regular practice, things get better and easier. It is time to start practising mindfulness. As mentioned before, go easy on yourself and be considerate. You will get there in a timely manner, this is a marathon, not a sprint to the finish line.

Mindful Breathing

Steps:

1. Find a comfortable position. You can sit on a chair, lie down, or sit on a mat.
2. Close your eyes or soften your gaze
3. Focus on your breath, noticing the inhale and exhale
4. When your mind wanders, gently bring it back to your breath
5. Start with 5 minutes and gradually increase the time that you exercise.

Interactive Element 2: Breath Awareness

Instructions:

1. Set a timer for 2 minutes.
2. Count your breaths, starting over each time your mind wanders.
3. Record your highest number before your mind starts to wander.

Highest breath count: _____

b) Body Scan

Steps:

1. Lie down or sit comfortably
2. Close your eyes
3. Slowly focus your attention on each part of your body, from your toes to your head
4. Note any sensations you are feeling without trying to change them
5. If your mind wanders, gently bring it back to the body part you were focusing on, refocus and continue.

c) Mindful Observation

Steps:

1. Choose an object in your environment
2. Observe it for 5 minutes. Examine it as if you are seeing it for the first time
3. Notice its colours, textures, soft or hard shapes, and any other characteristics it may have
4. If your mind wanders, gently bring it back to focus on the object

Interactive Element 3: Mindful Observation Journal

Instructions: Practice mindful observation with an everyday object of your choice. Examine the object and write down five new things you noticed about it.

Object: _____

MINDFULNESS IN DAILY LIFE

Mindfulness is something that you can use whenever and wherever you are. It isn't just for reflection and quiet moments. It is your superpower, goes with you everywhere, and is available anytime.

Everyday mindfulness practices:

- Mindful eating: Pay attention to the characteristics of your food, the taste, texture, and smell of your food.
- Mindful walking: Focus on the sensation of your feet touching the ground, how your body feels, and any sensations you may have.
- Mindful listening: Give your full attention to the person speaking without planning your response or feeling you want them to hurry up and finish. Be present and non-judgmental with no preconceived ideas.
- Mindful chores: Bring full awareness to routine tasks like washing dishes, hoovering, shopping or folding the laundry.

Interactive Element 4: Mindful Moment Tracker

Instructions: This can be done at home or work and will only take a few minutes. For a day over 8 hours, set reminders to practice mindfulness every 2-3 hours (you can use your phone to do this or any alarm that you find more convenient. Note what you were doing and how it felt to bring mindfulness to that activity.

Time	Activity	Experience
8:00 am		
10:00 am		
12:00 pm		
2:00 pm		
4:00 pm		
6:00 pm		
8:00 pm		

MINDFULNESS FOR ANXIOUS THOUGHTS:

When situations get tense and you begin to experience anxious thoughts, mindfulness can be helpful and come to your aid, "your lifeboat at sea".

Techniques:

A. **Thought Labelling:** Note "thinking" when you notice a thought, then return to your breath
B. **Leaves on a Stream:** Imagine placing each thought on a leaf and watching it float away
C. **Thank Your Mind:** Acknowledge the thought by saying "Thanks, mind" and simply let it go.
D. **STOP Technique:** Stop what you're doing. Take a breath. Observe your thoughts, feelings and sensations. Proceed with awareness.

Interactive Element 5: Thought Observation

Instructions:

1. Set a timer for a full 5 minutes.

2. Observe your thoughts, but do not engage with your thoughts.

3. Note the type of thoughts you noticed you were having.

Type of thoughts observed:

☐ Worries about the future:

☐ Regrets about the past:

☐ Self-critical thoughts:

☐ Planning or problem-solving:

MINDFULNESS AND ANXIETY

☐ RANDOM MEMORIES:

☐ Others:

LOVING-KINDNESS MEDITATION

Practising this next exercise will help you to prepare and use compassion. You will need to have compassion for yourself, and this can be a powerful remedy for anxiety.

Steps:

1. Find a spot where you will not be disturbed. Sit or lay comfortably and close your eyes.
2. Bring into your mind someone you care about or have recently had on your mind.
3. Silently repeat phrases like: "May you be safe", "May you be healthy", "May you live with ease."
4. Gradually extend these wishes to yourself, others, and finally to everyone.

Mindfulness takes practice and can sometimes seem difficult, but it is well worth the practice and the time you spend on it. You will successfully overcome the hurdles that you are presented with.

Challenges and solutions:

- **"I can't stop my thoughts":** The trick and the goal here is

to remember that you are not stopping your thoughts, you are observing them without judgment.
- **"I don't have time":** Do not stress yourself and get over-anxious, begin with a manageable 5 minutes a day, or practice between or during routine activities.
- **"I keep falling asleep":** If you do fall asleep, try practising at different times of the day or in a seated position; these could help keep you awake and focused.
- **"I'm not doing it right":** There's no "right" way to practice this type of meditation, and any amount of practice will benefit you greatly.

Interactive Element 6: Mindfulness Challenge Solver

Instructions: Identify one challenge you have faced with your mindfulness practice and think about three potential solutions.

What has been your challenge?

Solution 1:

Solution 2:

Solution 3:

[   ]

REFLECTING ON YOUR PROGRESS

We are now concluding this chapter. You have done so well!

Take a moment to think about and acknowledge how well you have done and how far you have come in the exploration of mindfulness and using mindfulness as a tool for managing your anxiety.

Interactive Element: Chapter Achievements

1. Write down one mindfulness technique that you found particularly helpful.

[   ]

2. How have you included a mindfulness plan into your daily routine?

[   ]

3. What one small win can you celebrate for being more present and mindful?

[   ]

Here we are now at the end of this chapter. It is now complete, and you have discovered how powerful mindfulness can be in helping to manage anxiety.

Chapter Summary:

Now that you have taken a deep dive into the awesome world of mindfulness, you must remember that mindfulness takes practice; it is a skill that grows more familiar and stronger when you use it regularly or often. Following this chapter, we will explore how lifestyle changes can continue to support your anxiety management journey. Transforming your life and daily habits will give you anxiety-busting superpowers.

Make a Difference with Your Review

UNLOCK THE POWER OF CALM

"Calmness is the cradle of power." – Josiah Gilbert Holland

When we give without expecting anything in return, we open ourselves to a sense of peace and purpose. Imagine if your words could help someone take the first step toward feeling calm and in control. That's the gift of a review.

Would you help someone just like you—curious about easing their anxiety but unsure where to start?

My mission with *Anxiety Released* is to make understanding and managing anxiety feel clear, approachable, and even empowering.

But to reach more people, I need your help.

Most people choose books based on reviews. By sharing your thoughts, you're helping another reader feel ready to take that first step toward calm. Your review could help…

…one more friend understand their worry and not feel alone. …one more student conquer fears in school. …one more parent find peace of mind. …one more teen discover the tools to calm their racing thoughts. …one more person break free from the grip of anxiety.

Making a difference is easy! Just scan the QR code below and leave a review:

If you love helping others, you're my kind of person. Thank you from the bottom of my heart!

—Olivia J Patterson

Higher Level Publishing

CHAPTER 7
LIFESTYLE CHANGES FOR ANXIETY MANAGEMENT

Welcome to the next chapter on your journey; in this chapter, we are going to explore how small changes in your daily habits can have a significant impact on your anxiety levels. You won't be just managing your anxiety, you will be building a life that is less likely to be influenced or harmed by your anxiety.

SLEEP HYGIENE

Getting good quality sleep is like pressing a reset button for your body and brain. We must ensure we hit that button regularly and get the best reset possible.

Key principles of sleep hygiene:

- Consistent sleep schedule (going to bed and waking up at the same time each day)
- Creating a relaxing bedtime routine (comfortable and clean bedding and a good sleep environment.)
- Optimizing your sleep environment (ensuring limits to outside noise and outside distractions.

- Limiting screen time before bed (turn off all blue lights and T.V.'s well before bedtime.)
- Avoiding caffeine and alcohol close to bedtime (avoiding stimulants that may affect your sleep)

It is well known that a lack of sleep can increase anxiety levels by as much as 30% as the brain's anticipatory reaction is very much heightened.

Interactive Element 1: Sleep Detective

Instructions: Track your sleep habits for at least a week and rate your anxiety levels each day, rating your levels on a scale of 1-10.

Day	Hours of Sleep	Bedtime	Wake Time	Anxiety Level (1-10)
Mon				
Tue				
Wed				
Thu				
Fri				
Sat				
Sun				

At the end of the week, reflect on any patterns you notice between your sleep habits and anxiety levels.

1. **Nutrition and Anxiety**

Have you heard the saying" You are what you eat"? This is true for your body, but it is also true for your mind and your mental state. Let's give your body some fuel that will calm your mind.

Anxiety-reducing foods:

- Complex carbohydrates (whole grains, peas, beans and vegetables)

LIFESTYLE CHANGES FOR ANXIETY MANAGEMENT

- Foods rich in magnesium (leafy greens, oysters, oats, nuts, spinach, avocado, seeds)
- Foods high in zinc (beef, oats, egg yolks, cashews)
- Omega-3 fatty acids (fatty fish, seafood, plant oils, flaxseed, chia seeds)
- Probiotic-rich foods (yogurt, kefir, pickles, Tempeh, cottage cheese, sauerkraut)

Foods to limit:

- Refined sugars
- Alcohol
- Caffeine
- Processed foods

Interactive Element 2: Mood Food Diary

Instructions: For three days, record what you eat and your anxiety levels. Notice if there are any patterns.

Day Breakfast Lunch Dinner Snacks Anxiety (1-10)

Day	Breakfast	Lunch	Dinner	Snacks	Anxiety Level (1-10)
1					
2					
3					

Reflections on food-mood connections:

1. Exercise as an Anxiety Reducer

We all know that movement and exercise are good for your body, but did you know they are also perfect for your overall well-being? They are also very powerful anxiety busters.

Benefits of exercise for anxiety:

- Releases endorphins, the body's natural mood elevators
- Reduces muscle tension
- Improves your quality of sleep
- Helps to boost self-esteem and cognitive function
- If you have problems and worries, exercise can be a healthy distraction

Types of exercise for anxiety:

- Aerobic exercises (running, cycling, swimming)
- Tai Chi
- Strength training
- Yoga
- Dance
- Pilates

Interactive Element 3: Movement Mood Booster

Instructions: Try a different type of exercise each day for a week. Rate your anxiety levels before and after.

LIFESTYLE CHANGES FOR ANXIETY MANAGEMENT

Day	Exercise Type	Duration	Anxiety Before (1-10)	Anxiety After (1-10)
Mon				
Tue				
Wed				
Thu				
Fri				
Sat				
Sun				

Write down which exercises that you recorded had the most significant impact on your anxiety.

TIME MANAGEMENT AND PRODUCTIVITY

There are times when life can be overwhelming, and these feelings of overwhelm can fuel your anxiety. One of the ways to avoid the feeling of overwhelm is to get organized and to take control of how you spend your time, this gives your time order and structure leaving less time for worry and anxiety.

Time management techniques:

- Prioritization (Eisenhower Matrix)
- Time blocking
- Pomodoro Technique
- To-do lists and goal-setting
- Reducing procrastination

INTERACTIVE ELEMENT 4: PRIORITY PLANNER

Instructions: List your tasks for tomorrow and categorize them using the Eisenhower Matrix.

Example:

Urgent and Important	Important but Not Urgent
1. Call doctor to discuss medication side effects	1. Start a daily meditation practice
2. Prepare for tomorrow's job interview	2. Plan a self-care routine for the week
3. Complete overdue work project	3. Research local support groups for anxiety
4. Pay overdue therapy bill	4. Schedule a catch-up with a supportive friend
Urgent but Not Important	**Neither Urgent nor Important**
1. Respond to non-critical emails	1. Scroll through social media
2. Attend optional team meeting	2. Reorganize bookshelf
3. Run errands for a friend	3. Watch new TV series
4. Return library books	4. Browse online shopping sites

Urgent and Important	Important but Not Urgent
1)	1)
2)	2)
3)	3)
4)	4)
Urgent but Not Important	**Neither Urgent nor Important**
1)	1)
2)	2)
3)	3)
4)	4)

Social Connections and Support Systems

Humans overall are very social and interactive creatures. We like to build and try to maintain healthy relationships that can help us socialize and reduce anxiety significantly.

LIFESTYLE CHANGES FOR ANXIETY MANAGEMENT

Benefits of social support:

- Provides a sense of belonging and self-worth
- Offers different perspectives on problems
- Acts as a buffer against stress
- Encourages healthy behaviours

Ways to strengthen your social connections:

- Regular check-ins with friends and family
- Joining clubs or groups based on interests
- Volunteering
- Seeking professional support when needed

Interactive Element 5: Connection Reflection

Instructions: Think carefully about your social support system.

List the names of three people that you can rely on for support:

List one thing that you can do this week that will strengthen your social connections:

Mindful Technology Use

The time is now, and we are in a digital age, so using technology with mindful consideration is essential for managing anxiety. Reduce the amount of negative information you take in, as this kind of information can act as fuel for anxiety.

Tips for mindful technology use:

- Set boundaries for the amount of time you use devices
- Practice digital detoxes (periods when you do not use digital devices)
- Use apps mindfully (consider anxiety-reduction apps and anxiety trackers)
- Be aware of social media's impact on your mood (reduce or eliminate the use of or interaction with harmful content)
- Limit exposure to anxiety-inducing news, information, friends and media

Interactive Element 6: Digital Detox Challenge

Instructions: Choose one day this week for a "digital detox." Record your experience.

Date of my digital detox:

Activities I did instead of using technology:

My feelings during the detox:

LIFESTYLE CHANGES FOR ANXIETY MANAGEMENT

My feelings after the detox:

CREATING AN ANXIETY-FRIENDLY ENVIRONMENT

Depending on how your space is organized, your environment can either help to reduce or help to fuel your anxiety. Make your space benefit and work for you!

Tips for an anxiety-friendly environment:

- De-clutter your space (a cluttered space is a cluttered mind)
- Incorporate calming colours (blues, violet, yellows, greens)
- Bring in natural elements (plants, natural light)
- Create a designated relaxation space (for reading, relaxing, and meditating)
- Use aromatherapy sticks or candles (lavender, chamomile)

Interactive Element 7: Calm Space Creator

Instructions: List five elements that you would include if you were to design your ideal space for reducing anxiety:

1	
2	
3	
4	
5	

List one change you can make to your environment this week:

REFLECTING ON YOUR PROGRESS:

As we end this chapter, consider and acknowledge the lifestyle changes you have thought about making for your anxiety management.

Interactive Element: Chapter Achievements

1. What's one lifestyle change you've made or plan to make?

2. How do you think this change will impact your anxiety levels?

3. Regarding improving and managing your lifestyle and anxiety levels, what is a win you can celebrate?

Another chapter is complete. You must congratulate yourself on getting this far and completing this chapter, You are taking steps towards a better lifestyle that supports you and how you manage your anxiety.

Chapter Summary:

You've just explored several lifestyle changes that are invaluable, and can seriously have a significant impact on your anxiety levels. Remember, small, consistent changes can lead to a much bigger impacting result over time. In the upcoming chapter, we'll dive into

LIFESTYLE CHANGES FOR ANXIETY MANAGEMENT

some relaxation techniques that can complement these lifestyle changes. By the end of the next chapter, you will be a relaxation expert!

CHAPTER 8
RELAXATION TECHNIQUES

Relaxation is like a retreat for your mind. In this chapter, we will explore the techniques that will help your body relax and your mind become calm. Relaxation is a skill that you can not only learn but master. The more you practice the better you will be at calming your mind and your anxiety.

THE SCIENCE OF RELAXATION

Let's take a look and see how relaxing can work on your body and your mind.

How relaxation affects the body:

- Activates the parasympathetic nervous system (allows the body to rest)
- Lowers heart rate and blood pressure
- Reduces muscle tension
- Slows your breathing rate
- Decreases the production of stress hormones

RELAXATION TECHNIQUES

Benefits for anxiety:

- Counteracts the fight-or-flight response
- Improves emotional regulation
- Thought process is clearer
- Boosts the immune function
- Improves your quality of sleep

Regular relaxation can change your brain structure; this increases the brain's Gray matter in areas associated with emotion and emotional regulation.

1. Deep Breathing Exercises

Breathing is like a remote control for your nervous system. Let's learn how to use it effectively!

Diaphragmatic Breathing:

1. Place one hand on your chest and the other on your belly
2. Breathe in slowly through your nose, feeling your belly expand
3. Exhale slowly through your mouth, your belly should now contract
4. Repeat this exercise for 5-10 minutes

4-7-8 Breathing:

1. Exhale entirely through your mouth
2. Close your mouth and inhale through your nose for four counts
3. Hold your breath for seven counts
4. Exhale entirely through your mouth for eight counts
5. Repeat for four cycles

Interactive Element 1: Breath Awareness Challenge

Instructions: Practice each breathing technique for a minimum of 5 minutes. Rate your anxiety levels before and after the exercise.

Technique	Anxiety Before (1-10)	Anxiety After (1-10)
Diaphragmatic		
4-7-8		

Which technique did you find more effective? Why?

PROGRESSIVE MUSCLE RELAXATION (PMR)

Progressive muscle relaxation is like giving yourself a full-body massage anytime, anywhere.

Steps:

1. Find a comfortable position either seated or lying down.

2. Starting with your toes, tense the muscles for 5 seconds

3. Release the tension and notice the feeling of relaxation

4. Move up through each muscle group (feet, legs, hips, abdomen, back, hands, arms, shoulders, neck, face)

5. Finish by tensing the whole of your body, then releasing

RELAXATION TECHNIQUES

Interactive Element 2: Tension Tracker

Instructions: As you practice PMR, note any areas of tension in your body.

Body Area	Tension Level (1-10)
Feet	
Legs	
Hips	
Abdomen	
Back	
Hands	
Arms	
Shoulders	
Neck	
Face	

Reflection: What did you notice about the tension in your body?

1. Guided Imagery

Guided imagery is relaxing and can be like a mini break for your mind. It is a time when you can find and develop a happy place so that you can transport yourself there anytime you choose.

Steps:

1. Find a quiet and comfortable space where you can sit or lie down
2. Close your eyes and take a few deep breaths (5-10)
3. Imagine a peaceful, safe place (This can be a real place or an imaginary place)
4. Engage all your senses in the visualization (what do you see, hear, smell, feel, taste?)
5. Spend 5-10 minutes exploring this place
6. When ready, slowly bring your awareness back to the present

Interactive Element 3: Imagery Creation

Instructions: Design your peaceful place for guided imagery.

What do you see?

What do you hear?

What do you smell?

RELAXATION TECHNIQUES

What do you feel?

What do you taste?

Practice visualizing this place for 5 minutes. How do you feel afterwards?

1. Autogenic Training

Your body is like a well-built computer; autogenic training is the same as programming your computer/body for relaxation.

Steps:

1. Find a comfortable position and sit or lie down, close your eyes

2. Repeat each of these phrases to yourself, focusing on the sensation:

- "My arms are heavy and warm"
- "My legs are heavy and warm"
- "My heartbeat is calm and regular"
- "My breathing is slow and relaxed"

- "My abdomen is warm"
- "My forehead is cool"

3. Repeat the cycle 3-6 times

It will take a while to get used to this exercise, and of course, you will have to keep your eyes open until you have memorized each phrase. Once you have practised a few times, you will likely find the process comfortable and rewarding.

Interactive Element 4: Autogenic Awareness

Instructions: Practice autogenic training. Rate how effectively you could create each sensation.

Sensation	Effectiveness (1-10)
Arm Heaviness and Warmth	
Leg Heaviness and Warmth	
Calm Heartbeat	
Slow Breathing	
Warm Abdomen	
Cold Forehead	

Which sensation was easiest to create? Which was most challenging?

1. Mindfulness Meditation

Mindfulness meditation allows you to be present and focused on what you are doing, saying and feeling. It is like giving your attention muscle a good workout.

RELAXATION TECHNIQUES

Steps:

1. Sit down comfortably with your back in an upright position
2. Focus your attention on your breath
3. When your mind wanders, gently bring it back to your breath
4. Start with 5 minutes and gradually increase

Interactive Element 5: Meditation Minutes

Instructions: Practice mindfulness meditation daily for a week and Record your experience.

Day	Duration	Ease of Focus (1- 10)	Anxiety Level After (1- 10)
Mon			
Tue			
Wed			
Thu			
Fri			
Sat			
Sun			

Reflection: How did your experience change over the week?

7. Body Scan

The body scan can be very revealing as it shines a light, brightening up areas of tension in your body that you may not have noticed or been aware of before.

1. Lie down or sit comfortably
2. Close your eyes and take a few deep breaths
3. Bring your attention to your toes, be aware of any sensations
4. Slowly move your attention up through your body, pausing and taking a moment at each part of the body
5. If you notice tension, take the time to breathe into that area and imagine it becoming more relaxed.
6. Continue until you've scanned your body from head to toe or toe to head.

Interactive Element 6: Body Awareness Map

Instructions: After practising a body scan, make a note of the areas where you noticed tension :

Reflection: Were you surprised by any areas of tension?

CREATING A RELAXATION ROUTINE

Having a routine for your relaxation is very important to how you are able to cope and manage stress and anxiety. The equivalent is taking a daily multivitamin for your mental health.

RELAXATION TECHNIQUES

Tips for creating a routine:

- Choose a consistent time, preferably the same time each day
- Start with 5-10 minutes, and over time, you can gradually increase the time you spend doing the exercises.
- Experiment with different techniques until you find one that you resonate with or that works best for you
- Create a relaxing environment (dim lights, water, comfortable seating, reduced noise, etc.)
- Be patient and persistent it may not be so easy at first but relaxation is a skill that improves with practice, just keep going.

Interactive Element 7: My Relaxation Prescription

Instructions: Design your personal relaxation routine.

Day	Time	Duration	Technique	Environmental Factor	Reminder
Mon					
Tue					
Wed					
Thu					
Fri					
Sat					
Sun					

REFLECTING ON YOUR PROGRESS

We are coming to the end of this chapter, take a moment to reflect and acknowledge what you have learned. Think about one relaxation technique that you have practised.

Interactive Element: Chapter Achievements

1. Which relaxation technique did you find most effective?

2. How will you make relaxation a part of your daily/regular routine?

3. Now that you have used relaxation to help manage anxiety, what small win can you celebrate?

Congratulations, this chapter is now complete, and you should be very proud of yourself. You have added powerful relaxation tools to your anxiety management tool kit. The skills you have learnt will prove to be invaluable.

Chapter Summary:

Well done, on adding a new technique to your tool kit, your understanding has increased and with regular practice your success is guaranteed as you go from strength to strength. You will be able to manage anxiety in any situation.

CHAPTER 9
EXPOSURE THERAPY

Onwards and upwards, you are here at last, this is the courage zone. This chapter is necessary as we will explore the topic of exposure therapy. This can be a powerful technique for facing your problems and fears head-on. What you should try to remember is that avoidance can help to feed your anxiety, but facing your fears and dealing with the issues shrinks the problems, fears and issues.

UNDERSTANDING EXPOSURE THERAPY

A good mental and physical workout can improve your anxiety and mental well-being. Exposure therapy is like weight training for your courageous muscles. At first, it will be uncomfortable, there will be some burning and stress on your muscles but it all adds to strengthening those muscles over time.

Key principles:

- "Small bursts of exposure to situations or objects of fear.
- "Allow the situation to continue until the anxiety levels go down or subside.

- "Understanding and acknowledging that the anxiety that you feel will subside over time.
- "Realizing that the worry and the feared outcome have no basis or truth.

Benefits:

- Reduces instances of avoidance behaviours
- Increases confidence with coping strategies and abilities.
- Provides realistic experience and evidence that overrides pre-existing anxious thoughts.
- Desensitizes the fear response over a period of time

Exposure therapy has proven to be one of the most successful evidence-based treatments for anxiety disorders, with success rates of 60-90% depending on the specific phobia or anxiety type.

TYPES OF EXPOSURE THERAPY

A. In Vivo Exposure: Direct, real-life exposure to feared situations or objects
B. Imaginal Exposure: Vividly imagining the feared situation
C. Virtual Reality Exposure: Using V.R. technology to simulate feared scenarios
D. Interoceptive Exposure: Inducing feared physical sensations (e.g., rapid heartbeat)

Interactive Element 1: Exposure Explorer

Instructions: For each type of exposure, think about and list how it might apply to one of your anxieties.

Anxiety:

In Vivo Exposure idea:

Imaginal Exposure idea:

Virtual Reality Exposure idea:

Interoception Exposure idea:

Which type of exposure seems most manageable to start with? Why?

CREATING AN EXPOSURE HIERARCHY

An exposure hierarchy is like a personalized roadmap for facing your fears, it tells you where to go next and how the strategies can help you.

. . .

Steps to create a hierarchy:

1. Identify the feared situation or object

2. Break it down into smaller, manageable steps

3. Rate each step on a scale of 0-100 for anxiety level

4. Arrange steps from least to most anxiety-provoking

Interactive Element 2: My Exposure Hierarchy

Instructions: Create an exposure hierarchy for one of your anxieties.

The anxiety is:

Step	Description	Anxiety Level (0-100)
1		
2		
3		
4		
5		
6		
7		
8		

IMPLEMENTING EXPOSURE EXERCISES

Now it's time to put your hierarchy into action and make it work for you. Remember to take your time and don't rush the process. In this instance, "slow and steady wins the race!"

EXPOSURE THERAPY

Guidelines for exposure:

- Start with the least anxiety-provoking item on your hierarchy
- Stay in the situation until your anxiety decreases by at least half
- Practice regularly (aim for 3-4 times a week)
- Use coping strategies (deep Breathing, positive self-talk, etc.) during exposure
- Gradually move up your hierarchy as you become more comfortable and confident

Interactive Element 3: Exposure tracker

Instructions: Track your progress with exposure exercises over a week and record your results in the table below.

Day	Exposure Exercise	Initial Anxiety (0-100)	Final Anxiety (0-100)	Time Spent
Mon				
Tue				
Wed				
Thu				
Fri				
Sat				
Sun				

Your thoughts about your progress:

COPING WITH DISCOMFORT DURING EXPOSURE

Discomfort can feel a little scary, making you wonder, "Why am I doing this?" but that is just your mind trying to protect you. A little fear is good for you, and a little discomfort is a natural part of exposure therapy. Read on to find the tools that will equip you to manage the discomfit.

Coping strategies:

- "Deep breathing
- "Positive self-talk
- "Practising Mindfulness techniques
- "Progressive muscle relaxation
- "Visualizing successful moments or scenes

Interactive Element 4: Coping Toolbox

Instructions: List your top 5 coping strategies for managing discomfort during exposure.

1	
2	
3	
4	
5	

Practice: Choose one strategy and describe how you will incorporate the strategy in your next exposure exercise.

OVERCOMING COMMON CHALLENGES IN EXPOSURE THERAPY

No matter who you are, even the bravest among us can face obstacles and moments of uncertainty or doubt. The hurdles are common ones, at the time when they come out they just don't feel common, they feel very individual. Let's get ready to remove some of those hurdles.

Challenges and solutions:

- Fear of panic: Remember, panic is temporary, and it will not harm you
- Difficulty staying in the situation: Use distraction techniques to manage the problem or bring a support person
- Lack of motivation: Remember to remind yourself of your goals and the benefits of facing your fears
- Setbacks: View them as learning opportunities, not failures, note them and move on from them. Do not linger in the emotion.

Interactive Element 5: Challenge Solver

Instructions: Identify a potential challenge in your exposure journey and brainstorm three possible solutions for overcoming these challenges.

What is the challenge?

Solution 1:

Solution 2:

_____

Solution 3:

_____

CELEBRATING SUCCESS AND MAINTAINING PROGRESS

No matter how small it is every success and every step forward you make is a step in the right direction. It all counts towards your success and victory, which is well worth celebrating.

Tips for maintaining progress:

- Keep practising, even after you have had initial success, keep building on your success.
- Gradually expose yourself to more challenging situations, think about how you will manage it and what techniques you will use, visualize, think about the benefits and go for it!
- Use the skills that you have learned in real-life situations.
- Keep a journal of your successes and learnings. Congratulate yourself and celebrate your wins.

Interactive Element 6: Victory journal

Instructions: Record three exposure-related successes you have had, no matter how small.

_____
_____
_____

How will you celebrate these victories?

| |
| |

WHEN TO SEEK PROFESSIONAL HELP

Self-guided exposure can be very effective, but professional support can sometimes benefit you in various ways.

Signs that you might benefit from professional help:

- Severe anxiety significantly impairs you from functioning daily.
- Difficulty progressing through your hierarchy
- The presence of other mental health issues or concerns (e.g., depression)
- Needing more structured support and guidance

Professionals who can help:

- Cognitive-behavioural therapists (CBT)
- Clinical psychologists
- Psychiatrists (for prescribed medication, if it is required)

Interactive Element 7: Professional support checklist

Instructions: Review the following statements and tick the ones that apply to you.

☐ Feelings of anxiety severely impact my daily life.

☐ I struggle to make progress with self-guided exposure.

☐ I have other mental health concerns that along with my anxiety is affecting me.

☐ I need a bit more support and guidance.

☐ I am thinking about prescribed medication as an option.

If you ticked any of these boxes, consider discussing professional support with your healthcare provider.

REFLECTING ON YOUR PROGRESS

As we come to the end of this chapter, I want you to take a moment to think about how far you have already come on this journey, acknowledge how much you have learned and how you now feel about managing your anxiety. You have shown great courage in considering and learning about exposure therapy.

Interactive Element: Chapter Achievements

What is one insight you have gained about facing your fears?

What one small step have you taken or plan to take which will help in facing a fear?

Regarding building the courage to face anxious situations, what is one small win you can celebrate?

You have done very well in completing this chapter. Congratulations on taking the brave steps that you needed to take to overcome your fears.

Chapter Summary:

You are a brave soul, and I salute you. You have just looked at and delved into the powerful world of exposure therapy. Facing your fears is a journey, not a destination. Take your time on this journey and celebrate every step that moves you forward, no matter how small the step may seem. You are doing so well! The next chapter will explore specific strategies for managing anxiety in various real-life situations. Get ready to become an anxiety-busting pro.

CHAPTER 10
ANXIETY IN SPECIFIC SITUATIONS

You have arrived, here you will find your very own personalized anxiety-busting tool kit. We will explore strategies for managing anxiety in common everyday challenging situations. You are not alone on this journey and you are not alone in facing these challenging situations, but with the right tools, you will be able to navigate them successfully.

SOCIAL ANXIETY

Social anxiety is similar to having a very, some may say, overly cautious internal bodyguard. We are going to teach that bodyguard to relax a little.

Key strategies:

Cognitive restructuring of social fears:

- Identify negative thoughts: "Everyone will think I'm dull and boring."
- Challenge these thoughts: "Do I have evidence for this? Have people said this?"

ANXIETY IN SPECIFIC SITUATIONS

- Replace with balanced thoughts: "Some people might find me interesting, others might not, that is normal."

Gradual exposure to social situations:

- Start small: Begin with brief interactions, like greeting a neighbour.
- Gradually increase the difficulty: move on to conversations that are a little longer. Then small gatherings, and eventually you will get to larger social events.
- Use a social situation hierarchy: Rate situations from least anxious to most anxiety-provoking and systematically work through each of them.

Mindfulness in social interactions:

- Focus on the present moment: Pay attention to what's being said rather than worrying about what you want to say next.
- "Practice active listening: This shifts focus from self-consciousness to genuine engagement and being present and in the moment.
- "Observe without judgment: Notice anxious feelings without trying to change them.

Focusing outward instead of on internal sensations:

- Use the "5-4-3-2-1" grounding technique: Identify five things you can see, four things you can touch, three things you can hear, two things you can smell, and one thing you can taste.
- Engage in the environment: Ask questions about your surroundings or the other person's interests, or work life. Hobbies is a topic people like to discuss.
- Practice curiosity: Approach social situations with a genuine interest in learning about others, ask questions that reflect your curiosity.

Practising social skills:

- Role-play conversations: Practice with a trusted friend or your therapist.
- Learn and use open-ended questions: These encourage longer, more engaging conversations.
- Practice non-verbal communication: Work on maintaining appropriate eye contact and body language that shows interest in what the other person is saying.

Interactive Element 1: Social Situation Ladder

	Situation	Anxiety Level (0-100)
1		
2		
3		
4		
5		

Choose one situation from your list to practice this week.

How will you prepare?

PERFORMANCE ANXIETY

Performance anxiety is experienced by many in various situations. The anxiety can be like a very critical internal coach questioning what you do and for whom you can always do a little more and be a little better. Let's teach that coach to be more understanding and supportive.

Strategies:

a) Visualization of successful performance:

- Create a detailed mental image: Visualize yourself performing confidently and successfully, how will you feel when you get your desired outcome. Make your visualization detailed.
- Engage all senses: Imagine what you'll see, hear, and feel during a successful performance. Go all out to make this feel as sensationally real as possible.
- Practice regularly: Spend 5-10 minutes daily visualizing your desired successful situations.

b) Re-framing about nervous energy as excitement:

- Change your self-talk: Instead of "I'm so anxious," say "I'm excited about this opportunity"
- Focus on possibilities: Think about what could go well, not what could go wrong.
- Embrace the physical sensations: Recognize that excitement and anxiety can feel similar in the body.

c) Breathing techniques for calming nerves:

- Practice 4-7-8 Breathing: Inhale for 4 counts, hold for 7, exhale for 8
- Use the box breathing method before performances: Inhale, hold, exhale, and hold again, each for four counts.
- You can incorporate belly breathing: Place a hand on your belly and breathe deeply, feeling it rise and fall.

d) Progressive muscle relaxation before performances:

- Start with your toes: Tense and relax each muscle group, moving up to your head
- Use as a pre-performance ritual: Practice for 10-15 minutes before going on stage
- Combine with visualization: As you relax each muscle, imagine the stress and anxiety leaving your body.

e) Positive self-talk and affirmations:

- Create personal mantras: "I am well-prepared and capable" etc.
- Challenge negative self-talk: Replace "I'm going to get this all wrong" with "I've prepared well and will do the best I can."
- Use power poses: Stand in a confident posture while reciting your affirmations.

Interactive Element 2: Performance Preparation Plan

Instructions: Create a pre-performance routine to manage your anxiety.

HEALTH ANXIETY

Health anxiety can be quite worrying, and it is like having an overactive internal doctor constantly giving you conflicting advice and diagnoses. Let's teach that internal doctor to be more balanced in their diagnoses.

Techniques:

a) Challenging catastrophic health-related thoughts:

- Identify the thought: "This headache is continuous, it must be a brain tumour"

ANXIETY IN SPECIFIC SITUATIONS

- Examine the evidence: "Headaches are common and rarely indicate serious conditions"
- Consider alternative explanations: "I might be dehydrated, tired or stressed"
- · Develop a balanced thought: "While it's unlikely to be serious, I'll monitor it and see a doctor if it continues beyond a couple of days."

b) Limiting health-related internet searches:

- Set boundaries: Limit health-related searches to once a week for no more than 20 minutes, or if you feel able to cut down on your anxiety by cutting them out altogether.
- Use reliable sources: Stick to reputable medical websites, not forums or personal blogs.
- Practice urge surfing: When the urge to search arises, observe it without feeling the need to act on it.

c) Mindful body awareness without over-interpretation:

- Body scan practice: Regularly scan your body, noticing sensations without judgment.
- Differentiate sensation from interpretation: "I feel a twinge" vs "This twinge means something is seriously wrong."
- Practice acceptance: Acknowledge sensations without trying to change or eliminate them. They are what they are.

d) Regular check-ups for reassurance:

- Schedule regular check-ups: This provides a structured time for addressing any health concerns you may have, want to look at, or discuss.
- Prepare questions in advance: Write specific concerns to discuss with your doctor. This will ensure that you discuss everything you want to without leaving anything out.

- Trust medical professionals: Remind yourself of their expertise when anxiety arises.

e) Distraction techniques when health worries arise:

- Engage in absorbing activities: Puzzles, crafts, hobbies or reading can redirect your focus.
- Use the 5-4-3-2-1 grounding technique: Focus on your five senses to bring yourself into the present moment, and be mindful of your surroundings.
- Practice mindfulness meditation: Focus on your breath or a mantra to centre yourself and bring your awareness back into the moment.

Interactive Element 3: Health Anxiety Thought Record

Instructions: Fill out this thought record next time you experience health anxiety.

Situation:

Anxious thought:

ANXIETY IN SPECIFIC SITUATIONS

Evidence for:

Evidence against:

Balanced thought:

Anxiety level before (0-100): _____
Anxiety level after (0-100): _____

FINANCIAL ANXIETY

Financial anxiety is similar to having an internal panic-prone accountant constantly worrying and catastrophizing. We are going to help that accountant to develop a more balanced perspective!

Strategies:

- Creating and sticking to a budget
- Building an emergency fund, save what you can when you can, or have a specific amount that you can add to your savings on a weekly or monthly basis (depending on when you get paid)

- Educating yourself about personal finance. What is it about finance that you have always wanted to know? This would be an excellent time to begin to educate yourself.
- Challenging catastrophic financial thoughts.
- Seeking reliable, professional financial advice when and where needed.

Interactive Element 4: Financial Anxiety Action Plan

Instructions: Identify three steps you can take to address your financial anxiety.

1	
2	
3	

Which step will you take first?

When

TRAVEL ANXIETY

Travel anxiety is like having a backseat passenger who doesn't drive telling you the driver what you should be doing or pointing out hazards which you have already anticipated or have nothing to do with you. Let's help that backseat navigator embrace the adventure of the journey.

. . .

ANXIETY IN SPECIFIC SITUATIONS

Techniques:

· Thorough preparation and planning

· Visualization of successful travel experiences

· Grounding techniques for use during travel

· Gradual exposure to different aspects of travel

· Creating a comforting travel kit

Interactive Element 5: Travel Comfort Kit

Instructions: Design your ideal travel comfort kit for managing anxiety.

	Item	Purpose
1		
2		
3		
4		
5		

TEST AND EXAM ANXIETY

Can you imagine having an overly nervous internal student who is anxious about a test "Test anxiety" Let's help to make that student feel more prepared, capable and confident.

Strategies:

- Effective study techniques (e.g., spaced repetition, making time to study, having all equipment ready, active recall)
- Mindfulness practices for an improved level of focus.
- Positive visualization of successful test-taking. Affirmations and positive self-talk.

- Breathing exercises to help calm your anxiety if it arises during the test.
- Re-framing any anxious thoughts about your performance or how you will do it.

Interactive Element 6: Test Anxiety Tool kit

Instructions: Create your personal toolkit for managing test anxiety.

Before the test:

1	
2	
3	

During the test:

1	
2	

After the test:

1	
2	

RELATIONSHIP ANXIETY

Relationship anxiety is like having an overly suspicious internal love detective. Let's help that detective trust and enjoy the experience of relationships a little more.

Techniques:

· Communication skills for expressing needs and concerns

ANXIETY IN SPECIFIC SITUATIONS

- Mindfulness in relationships to stay present
- Challenging negative beliefs about relationships
- Building self-esteem independent of relationships
- Gradual exposure to vulnerability in relationships

Interactive Element 7: Relationship Anxiety Reflection

Instructions: Reflect on your relationship anxiety.

My primary relationship fear is?

Where does this fear come from?

What evidence challenges this fear?

What one step can I take to remove this fear?

GENERALIZED ANXIETY IN DAILY LIFE

Imagine having an overactive internal alarm system, it seems to go off whenever it wants to without rhyme or reason or addressing a real fear. Let's adjust that system to be more accurately tuned to turn on when there is a real threat.

Strategies:

- Worry time scheduling
- Problem-solving techniques for real vs. hypothetical worries
- Mindfulness practices for staying present
- Challenging cognitive distortions
- Regular relaxation practices

Interactive Element 8: Worry time log

Instructions: Schedule a 15-minute "worry time" each day for a week. Log your experience.

Day	Time	Main Worries	Resolution Ideas
Mon			
Tue			
Wed			
Thu			
Fri			
Sat			
Sun			

Reflection: How did scheduling worry time affect your anxiety throughout the day?

ANXIETY IN SPECIFIC SITUATIONS

| |
| |
| |

REFLECTING ON YOUR PROGRESS

As we conclude this chapter, take a moment to acknowledge your growing ability to understand and manage anxiety in specific situations.

Interactive Element: Chapter Achievements

1. Write down a strategy you have learned and found particularly useful.

| |
| |
| |

2. How do you plan to apply or have you applied this strategy yet?

| |
| |
| |

3. Regarding handling anxiety, what one small win can you celebrate?

| |
| |

Congratulations on completing this chapter and expanding your ability to manage anxiety across various life situations!

Chapter Summary:

Yippee! You've just equipped yourself with strategies that you can use to cope with and manage your anxiety in certain situations. Remember these strategies will take time and practice to make consistent progress. Remember to celebrate your wins, and be reassured if some techniques take a little longer to learn than others. Each time you use one of the techniques or strategies you have learned, you build your anxiety muscle and confidence.

In the next chapter, we will look at when and how to seek professional help for your anxiety. You have come this far, and you are doing just great!

CHAPTER 11
WHEN TO SEEK PROFESSIONAL HELP

At last, you are at the final step in your anxiety management journey. Self-help strategies are very powerful but sometimess we need a little expert guidance.

In this chapter we will look at when and how to seek professional help for your anxiety. Reaching out for help is not a sign of weakness, it is a sign of strength.

RECOGNIZING WHEN PROFESSIONAL HELP IS NEEDED

It can be hard to see the forest for the trees, and you wonder if there is a light at the end of the tunnel. Using this book's methods, strategies and techniques, there is always a light at the end of the tunnel. Let's learn to notice and understand when it is time to call a professional to help you get further along in your journey.

Signs that professional help may be beneficial:

Severity of symptoms:

- Anxiety can severely impact and interfere with daily life, work, relationships, hygiene, and self-care.

- Panic attacks are happening frequently or they are severe.
- You're avoiding important activities or places due to your feelings of anxiety or negative self-talk.

Duration of symptoms:

- Anxiety has persisted for several weeks, months or even longer.
- Symptoms are chronic or recurring.

Impact of function:

- Difficulty maintaining relationships due to your anxiety
- Work or academic performance is suffering as a result of your anxiety.
- Because of your anxiety, you are unable to enjoy activities you once loved.

Presence of other mental health concerns:

- Experiencing symptoms of depression alongside anxiety.
- Substance use to cope with anxiety.
- Thoughts of self-harm or suicide (For this, seek immediate help)

Ineffectiveness of self-help strategies:

- You have tried multiple self-help techniques and strategies and have seen no notable improvement.
- You are unclear on how to apply anxiety management techniques and strategies to your life or situation.

WHEN TO SEEK PROFESSIONAL HELP

Interactive Element 1: Professional Help Assessment

Instructions: Rate the following statements from 0, none, to 5 a lot

1. My anxiety interferes with my daily life: _____
2. I've been feeling anxious for several weeks or months: _____
3. My relationships or work are suffering due to anxiety: _____
4. I'm experiencing other mental health concerns alongside anxiety: _____
5. Self-help strategies haven't significantly improved my anxiety: _____

Total Score: (add questions number 1-5 to get your total score) _____

If your total score is 15 or higher, it may be beneficial for you to consider professional help for your anxiety issues.

TYPES OF MENTAL HEALTH PROFESSIONALS

There are many different types of mental health professionals, each with their fields of expertise. Here is information about the various health professionals and how they could help or support you.

Psychologists:

- Provide therapy and psychological testing.
- Does not prescribe medication.

Often specialize in specific types of therapy (e.g., CBT, exposure therapy)

Psychiatrists:

- Medical doctors who can prescribe medication.
- Some also provide therapy, but many focus on managing anxiety with medication.

Licensed professional counsellors (LPC):

- Counsellors provide therapy for many different mental health issues.
- Some will often take a holistic approach to mental health.

Licensed Clinical Social Workers (LCSW):

- Will provide therapy and help and let you know about accessing resources within the community.
- Will often work in hospitals or community health settings.

Psychiatric nurse practitioners:

- Can help to provide therapy and also prescribe medication.
- Will often take a holistic approach to mental health care.

Interactive Element 2: Professional Match

Instructions: Which type of professional would most appropriately be what you need?

My primary needs are (check all that apply):

☐ Therapy for Anxiety

☐ Medication evaluation

☐ Psychological testing

☐ Holistic approach to mental health

☐ Help accessing community resources and funds

WHEN TO SEEK PROFESSIONAL HELP

Based on these needs, I might benefit most from seeing a:

```
┌─────────────────────────────────────────────┐
│                                             │
└─────────────────────────────────────────────┘
```

TYPES OF THERAPY FOR ANXIETY

There are many different therapies for anxiety which can prove very effective. Let's explore some of the most common approaches.

Cognitive Behavioural Therapy (CBT):

- The aim is to identify and change negative thought patterns and behaviours.
- Highly effective for a number of anxiety disorders.
- Often includes homework assignments and skill-building.

Exposure Therapy:

- This technique involves gradual, controlled exposure to feared situations or objects.
- Particularly effective for specific phobias and OCD (Obsessive Compulsive Disorder)
- Can be a challenging process, but it is highly effective when completed.

Acceptance and Commitment Therapy (ACT):

- Based on accepting uncomfortable thoughts and feelings rather than fighting them.
- Focuses on value-based actions and mindfulness.
- Effective for various anxiety disorders and chronic worry.

Dialectical Behaviour Therapy (DBT):

- Combines CBT techniques with mindfulness and emotional self-regulation skills.

- Was developed for borderline personality disorder but very effective for anxiety.
- Focus is on balancing acceptance and change.

Psychodynamic Therapy:

- Explores how past experiences and unconscious thoughts influence current behaviour
- Can be longer term than other therapies
- May be particularly helpful for anxiety rooted in childhood experiences

Interactive Element 3: Therapy Exploration

Instructions: Research each type of therapy and rate your interest from 1 (low) to 5 (high).

CBT: _____

Exposure Therapy: _____

ACT: _____

DBT: _____

Psychodynamic Therapy: _____

Which therapy approach interests you most?

_____

Why?

MEDICATION OPTIONS FOR ANXIETY

Medication can be a helpful tool in managing anxiety. Let's learn about some of the more common options.

Note: Always consult a psychiatrist or primary care doctor about medication options.

Selective Serotonin Reuptake Inhibitors (SSRIs):

- Often the first-line medication for anxiety disorders
- Examples: Fluoxetine (Prozac), Sertraline (Zoloft), Escitalopram (Lexapro)
- May take several weeks to become fully effective

Serotonin-Norepinephrine Reuptake Inhibitors (SNRIs):

- Similar to SSRIs but affect two neurotransmitters
- Examples: Venlafaxine (Effexor), Fluoxetine (Cymbal ta)
- Can be effective for anxiety and depression

Benzodiazepines:

- Fast-acting anti-anxiety medications
- Examples: Alprazolam (Xanax), Lorazepam (Ativan)
- Generally for short-term use due to the risk of dependence

Buspirone:

- Anti-anxiety medication that is not habit-forming.
- It is often used for generalized anxiety disorder.
- May take several weeks to work and become effective.

Beta-Blockers:

- Can help with physical symptoms of anxiety (e.g., rapid heartbeat).

- More often used for performance anxiety. Examples: Propranolol, Atenolol

Interactive Element 4: Medication Considerations

Instructions: If and when you are considering medication, so that you remember everything, you should list your questions or concerns so that you can discuss them with your healthcare provider.

1	
2	
3	

Finding the right professional

Finding the right mental health care professional is like finding a good dance partner. It might take a few tries to find the right fit.

Steps to find a professional:

1. Check with your insurance provider for in-network options
2. Ask for recommendations from your primary care physician or trusted friends.
3. Use online directories (e.g., Psychology Today, Good Therapy)
4. Consider telehealth options for greater accessibility
5. Prepare questions for your first consultation.

Interactive Element 5: Professional Fit Checklist

Instructions: When meeting a new mental health professional, consider these factors:

☐ Do I feel comfortable opening up and talking to this person?

☐ Are they experienced in treating the type of anxiety that is specific to me?

WHEN TO SEEK PROFESSIONAL HELP

☐ Is their treatment approach one that I can get on board with?

☐ Is their location and office hours convenient for me?

☐ Do I get along with this person, am I being understood and heard?

1. Preparing for your first appointment

Your first appointment will be unfamiliar and new, and it will be like the opening chapter of a new book. Let's make sure that your first encounter is a good one.

Preparation tips:

- Write down your symptoms and concerns.
- Prepare a list of questions that you would like to ask.
- Bring relevant medical history or any relevant medication information.
- Be honest about your experiences and what you expect to achieve.
- It's okay to be nervous, take your time, and all will be well.

Interactive Element 6: First Appointment Prep

Instructions: Prepare for your first appointment by answering these questions:

1. What are my main anxiety symptoms?

| |
| |

2. When did these symptoms start?

| |
| |

3. What are my goals for therapy?

4. What questions do I have for the professional?

5. What hesitations or concerns do I have about starting therapy?

6. How will I combine Professional Help with Self-Help Strategies?

Professional help and self-help strategies are like ham and cheese, great on their own, but even better together.

Tips for integration:

- Share self-help strategies you've found helpful with your therapist.
- Ask how to incorporate therapy lessons into daily life.
- Continue practising mindfulness strategies and relaxation techniques.
- Maintain an anxiety journal to track your progress and identify any patterns.

WHEN TO SEEK PROFESSIONAL HELP

- Be patient with yourself, and healing is a process that combines professional guidance and personal input and effort.

Interactive Element 7: Integration Plan

Instructions: Create a plan to combine professional help with self-help strategies:

Professional: I will

| |
| |

Self-help strategy 1:

| |
| |

Self-help strategy **2:**

| |
| |

How will I track my progress?

| |
| |

REFLECTING ON YOUR PROGRESS:

As we conclude this chapter, take a moment to acknowledge your input and the hands-on steps you have taken to understand when and how to seek professional help.

Interactive Element: Chapter Achievements

1. Write down one significant sign that tells you it's time to seek professional help.

2. Has your perspective on professional help for anxiety changed?

3. How has your perspective changed?

Congratulations on completing this chapter and empowering yourself with knowledge about the various types of professional help and support available to those with anxiety.

Chapter Summary:

Congratulations on completing this journey into understanding and managing anxiety. Seeking professional help is taking a courageous step towards better mental health. Now you can acknowledge and recognize when professional help might be appropriate and beneficial. You also know how to find the right help and support.

WHEN TO SEEK PROFESSIONAL HELP

Keep using the self-help strategies you've learned, and don't hesitate to reach out to a mental health professional if and when you need to. You've got this!

CHAPTER 12
MAINTAINING PROGRESS AND PREVENTING RELAPSE

Welcome to the final chapter of your anxiety management journey. You've come so far; now it's time to learn how to maintain your progress and prevent relapse. Remember, managing anxiety is an ongoing process, not a destination."

UNDERSTANDING THE NATURE OF RECOVERY

Recovery from anxiety is like taking care of a pet that you love; it requires you to put in time, attention and care, but the feelings you get back in return are invaluable.

Key points:

· Your recovery will take more work. There will be starts, stops and setbacks; this is normal and should be expected.

· Your progress will come in small steps and waves as you go on the journey.

· Anxiety management is a skill that you can master, and it will improve with regular practice.

MAINTAINING PROGRESS AND PREVENTING RELAPSE

· Recovery doesn't mean never feeling anxious, It means having tools, techniques and strategies to cope with and manage your anxiety effectively.

Interactive Element 1: Recovery Reflection

Instructions: Reflect on your anxiety management journey so far.

1. What's the most significant change you've noticed?

2. What strategy has been most helpful?

3. What's still challenging for you?

4. What are you most proud of in your journey?

CREATING A MAINTENANCE PLAN

Having a maintenance plan is like a roadmap, you are on a journey, and you need to equip yourself with the right tools to know where to go and what to do along the way as you stay on the road and continue your anxiety management journey.

Components of a maintenance plan:

A. Regularly practice coping strategies and anxiety management techniques.
B. Identify personal triggers and warning signs so they can be managed.
C. Strategies and techniques for managing high-stress periods and situations.
D. Self-care routine must be included.
E. Consider what or who your support system will be and how you will use support when needed.
F. Continued goal setting and tracking your progress.

Interactive Element 2: My Maintenance Plan

Instructions: Draft your anxiety maintenance plan, including:

Daily practices:

Weekly practices:

MAINTAINING PROGRESS AND PREVENTING RELAPSE

My main triggers:

Warning signs to watch for:

Strategies for high-stress times:

Self-care activities:

My support system:

Next anxiety management goal:

RELAPSE PREVENTION STRATEGIES

Having a plan and getting ready to prevent relapse is like having a first aid kit available. It is best to think about how and what you will do in advance of having an emergency.

Key strategies:

Regular self-assessment:

- Conduct weekly "check-ins" with yourself to assess your anxiety levels and how you are.
- Use anxiety-tracking apps or journals to monitor symptoms over time. Reading over your journal weekly will give you insights.

Maintaining healthy habits:

- Prioritize your sleep and your sleep hygiene.
- Maintain a balanced diet.
- Engage in regular exercise.
- Do things to help you relax, such as hobbies, reading, art, etc.
- Practice stress-management techniques daily.

Continuing exposure:

- Regularly face anxiety-provoking situations to maintain your progress.
- Gradually increase the challenge level of exposure to situations.

Mindfulness practice:

- Incorporate daily mindfulness exercises
- Use mindfulness to catch anxiety symptoms early

MAINTAINING PROGRESS AND PREVENTING RELAPSE

Stress management:

- Use time-management techniques to prevent the feeling of overwhelm.
- Practice saying "no" to maintain a manageable schedule
- Use relaxation techniques whenever you want to, rather than only when feeling anxiety.

Interactive Element 3: Relapse Prevention Toolkit

Instructions: Create your personal relapse prevention toolkit.

Self-assessment method:

Healthy habits to maintain:

Exposure exercises to continue:

Daily mindfulness practice:

Stress management techniques:

RECOGNIZING AND MANAGING SETBACKS

Please note that setbacks are not failures, they are opportunities for learning, reflection and growth.

Steps for managing setbacks:

1. Recognize the setback without any judgment.
2. Identify potential triggers or contributing factors for the setback.
3. Review and apply relevant anxiety management strategies to help you cope and move forward.
4. Reach out for support from someone you trust or a professional if you need it.
5. Adjust your maintenance plan based on what you've learned.

Interactive Element 4: Setback Action Plan

Instructions: Create an action plan for managing setbacks.

Step 1: How will I recognize a setback?

Step 2: Key strategies to apply:

Step 3: Who will I reach out to for support?

MAINTAINING PROGRESS AND PREVENTING RELAPSE

Step 4: How might I need to adjust my maintenance plan?

```
┌─────────────────────────────────────────────────────────┐
│                                                         │
│                                                         │
└─────────────────────────────────────────────────────────┘
```

THE ROLE OF ONGOING SELF-EDUCATION

Continuing to learn about anxiety is like sharpening your tools, it keeps your skills effective and up-to-date. You can also add new techniques and strategies and take out ineffective ones that no longer work or that you do not resonate with.

Ways to continue learning:

- Read books and articles about anxiety and mental health.
- Attend workshops or webinars on anxiety management and mindfulness.
- Join support groups or online forums.
- Follow reputable mental health professionals on social media.
- Consider taking courses on stress management or mindfulness.

Interactive Element 5: Learning Plan

Instructions: Create a plan for ongoing anxiety education.

Book I want to read:

```
┌─────────────────────────────────────────────────────────┐
│                                                         │
└─────────────────────────────────────────────────────────┘
```

Workshop or course I'm interested in:

```
┌─────────────────────────────────────────────────────────┐
│                                                         │
└─────────────────────────────────────────────────────────┘
```

Support group or forum I might join:

[ ]

Mental health professional or organization I'll follow:

[ ]

CELEBRATING PROGRESS AND SUCCESS

Any celebration that makes you feel good and motivates you to continue your progress is good. The wins and the celebration will help to keep you going when times get tough.

Ways to celebrate progress:

- Keep a success journal to record victories, big and small.
- Share your progress with supportive friends or family.
- Reward yourself for reaching milestones in your anxiety management journey.
- Practice positive self-talk and self-acknowledgement.
- Regularly reflect on how far you've come.

Interactive Element 6: Success Celebration

Instructions: Plan how you'll celebrate your anxiety management progress.

1. Three successes I've had in managing my anxiety:

MAINTAINING PROGRESS AND PREVENTING RELAPSE

1	
2	
3	

2. How I'll celebrate these successes:

3. My next milestone:

4. How I'll reward myself when I reach it:

1. **Building resilience for long-term problem-solving success.**

Building resilience is similar to strengthening your emotional immune system, it helps you to bounce back from challenges quickly and more easily.

STRATEGIES FOR BUILDING RESILIENCE:

- Cultivate a growth mindset.
- Practice self-compassion regularly.
- Develop your problem-solving skills.
- Build and maintain strong social connections.
- Find purpose and meaning in daily life.
- Practice gratitude regularly (preferably daily)

Interactive Element 7: Resilience Builder

Instructions: Choose one resilience-building strategy to focus on this week.

Strategy I'll focus on:

How I will practice this strategy:

Day 1:

Day 2:

Day 3:

MAINTAINING PROGRESS AND PREVENTING RELAPSE

Day 4:

Day 5:

Day 6:

Day 7:

REFLECTING ON YOUR PROGRESS:

How did practising this strategy affect my overall well-being?

Chapter Summary:

Let me congratulate you. You are doing so well! What a journey this has been, It may have seemed such a long journey that at times you could hear your inner child screaming "Are we there yet?"

You have learned how to manage your anxiety. You have the toolbox filled with strategies, techniques and the know-how to manage and use them effectively. Now that you have come this far you now have to maintain the progress that you have made by building resilience. Resilience will help you keep going when times get tough and when you feel it's hard to keep going. Remember that managing your anxiety is an ongoing long-term process, and every step that you take is a victory and a win that should be celebrated. You have come far, and you should be proud. Keep using the techniques, strategies and methods you have learned to support you and to keep you growing. You've got this!

CHAPTER 13
CELEBRATING PROGRESS AND ACKNOWLEDGING ACHIEVEMENTS

THE IMPORTANCE OF ACKNOWLEDGING PROGRESS

In our journey to manage anxiety, we often focus so intently on our struggles that we overlook our victories. Acknowledging progress is a crucial component of successful anxiety management. Here's why:

1. Positive Reinforcement: Recognizing and celebrating your achievements reinforces positive behaviours, making it more likely you'll continue using effective strategies.

2. Boosting Motivation: Seeing progress, no matter how small, can motivate you to keep going when times get tough.

3. Building Self-Efficacy: Acknowledging your ability to cope and manage anxiety builds confidence in your ability to handle situations that may be challenging in the future.

4. Counteracting Negativity Bias: Anxiety usually involves focusing on the negative. Actively recognizing your progress will help balance this perspective.

OVERCOMING THE TENDENCY TO DISMISS PROGRESS

Many anxiety sufferers struggle to acknowledge and celebrate their achievements. This can be due to:

- Perfectionism: Setting unrealistically high standards for what counts as progress.
- Negative Self-Talk: Internal dialogue that downplays any achievements.
- Comparison: Measuring progress against others rather than your starting point.

To overcome these tendencies:

1. Challenge your thoughts: When you dismiss the progress you have made, ask, "If the situation was reversed, what would I say to a friend?"

2. Practice balanced thinking: Acknowledge the reality of both the struggle and the improvement.

3. Focus on personal growth: Do not compare yourself to where you were, not to others or an ideal standard. Instead, look at how far you have come on your journey.

Interactive Element: Progress Perspective Shift

Think of a recent situation where you managed your anxiety. Write down the answers to the following questions:

1. What did I do well in this situation?

CELEBRATING PROGRESS AND ACKNOWLEDGING ACHIEVEME...

2. How does this compare to how I would have handled it in the past?

```
_____
_____
_____
```

3. What does this success say about my ability to manage my anxiety?

```
_____
_____
_____
```

IDENTIFYING AND CELEBRATING SMALL WINS

In anxiety management, progress does not come all at once it takes time and comes in small shifts and movement towards progress. You must learn to recognize and celebrate these "small wins." It is an essential component of continued success. Here are a few examples:

- Using a breathing technique or another practised strategy during a stressful moment.
- Challenging a negative thought that might come up.
- Facing a minor fear.
- Practising self-care despite your feelings of anxiety.

Interactive Element: My Anxiety Management Victories

List five anxiety management achievements from the past week, no matter how small:

1	
2	
3	
4	
5	

Now for each achievement, write down why you feel it is significant:

1	
2	
3	
4	
5	

CELEBRATING PROGRESS AND ACKNOWLEDGING ACHIEVEME...

MEASURING PROGRESS OVER TIME:

Tracking your progress can provide concrete evidence that you are improving. Being able to see and read through your progress and see how far you have come is a great way of building confidence in your progress and your abilities.

Methods for tracking progress include:

1. **Anxiety Journals**: Record your daily anxiety levels and the coping strategies.
2. **Symptom Trackers:** Keep a record of how often and how intense specific anxiety symptoms are.
3. **Behaviour Logs:** Track the times you faced the fears and write down the management techniques used.
4. **Goal Achievement Records:** Track your progress towards specific anxiety management goals.

Interactive Element: My Progress Tracker

Create a simple graph to visualize your anxiety levels over the past month.

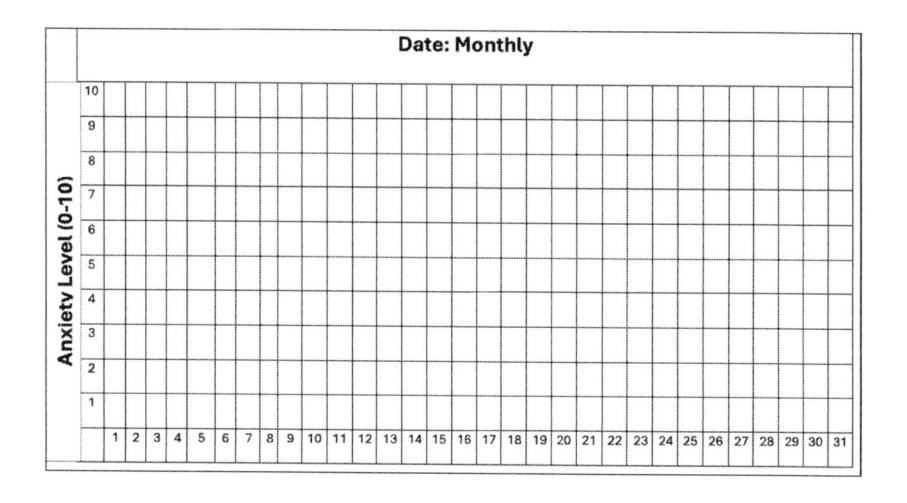

[Blank monthly graph — Date: Monthly — Anxiety Level (0-10) on y-axis from 1 to 10, days 1–31 on x-axis]

Think about any improvements or patterns you have noticed:

CELEBRATING ACHIEVEMENTS:

Celebrating your achievements reinforces your progress, builds confidence and capability, and encourages you to keep going and keep growing.

Ideas for celebration include:

1. Treat yourself to something you enjoy.

2. Share your success with a supportive friend or family member

3. Go somewhere you have always wanted to visit or have been curious about.

4. Write your achievement in a "success journal."

5. Practice positive self-talk, acknowledging the hard work you have done.

6. Have a "Rewards list" and choose something from the list.

7. Choose and do a favourite activity as a reward.

Interactive Element: My Celebration Plan

List three ways that you will celebrate achieving your next anxiety management milestone:

1	
2	
3	

CELEBRATING PROGRESS AND ACKNOWLEDGING ACHIEVEME...

Why did you choose these celebration methods?

```
┌─────────────────────────────────────────┐
│                                         │
│                                         │
│                                         │
└─────────────────────────────────────────┘
```

DEALING WITH SETBACKS

Setbacks are a normal part of any journey, and you will face a few. Now that you know how to build resilience, you will acknowledge the setback and see it as an opportunity to learn and grow while incorporating your anxiety management skills.

When you are faced with a setback:

1. **Practice self-compassion**: Be kind to yourself, as you would be to a friend.
2. **Reframe the setback:** View the setback as a learning opportunity, not a failure.
3. **Review your progress:** Look back at how far you've come.
4. **Assess and adjust your strategies:** Use setbacks to inform and improve your approach.

Interactive Element: Setback Reframe

Describe a recent setback in your anxiety management:

```
┌─────────────────────────────────────────┐
│                                         │
│                                         │
│                                         │
└─────────────────────────────────────────┘
```

Now, reframe this setback positively:

1. What can I learn from this experience?

[blank response box]

2. In what way can I use this to improve my anxiety management?

[blank response box]

3. What are the potential obstacles, and how will you overcome them?

[blank response box]

THE ROLE OF SELF-COMPASSION:

Self-compassion involves treating yourself with the same kindness you'd offer to someone else that you care about, such as a family member or a good friend. Treating yourself well and having self-compassion is vital for acknowledging your progress and maintaining motivation.

To practice self-compassion:

1. **Mindfulness:** Acknowledge how you are feeling without making any judgment.
2. **Common Humanity:** Know that struggles are something that every person faces and goes through.
3. **Self-kindness:** Speak to yourself using words of encouragement and understanding.

CELEBRATING PROGRESS AND ACKNOWLEDGING ACHIEVEME...

Interactive Element: Self-Compassion Letter

Write a brief, compassionate letter to yourself acknowledging your efforts in managing anxiety:

Dear (Your Name),

(Write your letter here, focusing on the progress of your efforts and offering words of kindness and encouragement)

Dear _____

SETTING FUTURE GOALS

As you acknowledge how far you have come, you must set new goals as you go along to allow for continued growth.

Use the SMART criteria:

- **S**pecific: Clearly define what you want to achieve.
- **M**easurable: Have a way to track your progress.
- **A**chievable: Ensure the goal is realistic, given your current situation.

- **R**elevant: The goal should align with your overall anxiety management plan.
- **T**ime-bound: Set a specific time frame for achieving the goal.

SMART OBJECTIVE EXAMPLE:

"I will practice mindful breathing for 10 minutes each day, five days a week, for the next month. I'll track my progress using a meditation app and aim to reduce my average daily anxiety level from 7 out of 10 to 5 out of 10 by the end of the month."

Let's break this down to show how it meets the SMART criteria:

Specific: The goal clearly states what will be done (mindful breathing), for how long (10 minutes), and how often (5 days a week).

Measurable: Progress can be tracked using a meditation app, and anxiety levels are measured on a scale of 1-10.

Achievable: 10 minutes of mindful breathing 5 days a week is a realistic goal for most people, even those new to the practice.

Relevant: Mindful breathing is directly related to anxiety management, making this goal relevant to the overall aim of reducing anxiety.

Time-bound: The goal has a clear timeframe of one month.

SMART Criteria	Objective Component
Specific	Practice mindful breathing for 10 minutes each day, five days a week
Measurable	Track progress using a meditation app; Reduce average daily anxiety level from 7 out of 10 to 5 out of 10
Achievable	10 minutes of practice, 5 days a week is realistic for most people
Relevant	Mindful breathing directly relates to anxiety management
Time-bound	Accomplish this goal over the next month

CELEBRATING PROGRESS AND ACKNOWLEDGING ACHIEVEME...

"This SMART objective provides a clear, actionable goal for incorporating mindfulness into your anxiety management routine. By setting specific parameters and a measurable outcome, you can easily track your progress and adjust your approach if needed. Remember, the key is to set goals that challenge you but remain achievable, helping you build confidence and motivation as you work towards managing your anxiety."

Interactive Element: My Next Anxiety Management Goals

List three SMART goals for your continued anxiety management journey:

1	
2	
3	

For each goal, explain:

"How you will measure your progress:

| |
| |
| |

Why this goal is important to you:

[ ]

Potential obstacles you may face and how you'll overcome them:

[ ]

Chapter Summary:

Acknowledging your progress and celebrating your achievements are vital to successful anxiety management. By recognizing how far you've come, tracking your progress, celebrating your wins, and setting future goals, you build the know-how, confidence and motivation to continue your anxiety management journey. Every step forward (no matter how small) is a victory worth celebrating. We will move on to the next chapter, where we will explore how to integrate all you've learned about anxiety management into your daily life.

CHAPTER 14
INTEGRATING ANXIETY MANAGEMENT INTO DAILY LIFE

Well here you are at the last and final chapter of your anxiety management journey. Here we are going to explore how to seamlessly weave the strategies you've learned into the fabric of your everyday life. Remember, true mastery comes from consistent, mindful practice in real-world situations.

CREATING AN ANXIETY FRIENDLY ROUTINE

Your daily routine can be your best and strongest helper and supporter when managing anxiety.

Below is a day designed to support your emotional well-being:

Key components of an anxiety-friendly routine are:

A. Consistent sleep schedule
B. Regular meals and hydration
C. Scheduled relaxation time
D. Exercise or physical activity
E. Mindfulness practice

F. Social connection
G. Productive work or study time
H. Taking time out to do leisure and hobbies.

Interactive Element 1: My Ideal Day

Instructions: Design your ideal anxiety-friendly day.

Time	Activity
6:00am	
8:00am	
10:00am	
12:00pm	
2:00pm	
4:00pm	
6:00pm	
8:00pm	
10:00pm	

Reflection: How does this ideal day differ from your current routine? What small changes can you implement this week?

MICRO-PRACTICES FOR ANXIETY MANAGEMENT

Micro-practices are like vitamins for your mental health small daily doses will add up over time and prove to have significant benefits.

Examples of micro-practices:

A. Take three deep breaths before checking emails
B. 2-minute mindfulness while waiting in a queue
C. Gratitude practice during your travel time (bus, train, tram.)
D. Body scan while brushing teeth

INTEGRATING ANXIETY MANAGEMENT INTO DAILY LIFE

   E. Positive affirmations while getting dressed
   F. 5-4-3-2-1 grounding technique during coffee breaks

Interactive Element 2: My Micro-Practice Plan

Instructions: Choose five micro-practices to implement in your daily life.

1. Morning micro-practice:

2. Work/study micro-practice:

3. Midday micro-practice:

4. Evening micro-practice:

5. Bedtime micro-practice:

6. Anxiety Management in the Workplace:

In terms of your work environment, being an efficient project manager for your emotions is similar to having the job of Anxiety Manager.

STRATEGIES FOR WORKPLACE ANXIETY MANAGEMENT:

- A. Time blocking for focused periods of work.
- B. Regular short breaks for relaxation or mindfulness.
- C. Setting realistic goals and boundaries.
- D. Using anxiety management techniques during stressful meetings or presentations.
- E. Creating a calming workspace for yourself.
- F. Communicate your needs with supervisors, management, or HR when appropriate.

Interactive Element 3: Workplace Anxiety Action Plan

Instructions: Create an action plan for managing anxiety at work.

What are your primary work-related anxiety triggers?

| |
| |

To manage these triggers, what are the strategies that will be used?

| |
| |

What I will do to create a more calming workspace:

| |
| |

INTEGRATING ANXIETY MANAGEMENT INTO DAILY LIFE

Who I can talk to if I need support:

ANXIETY MANAGEMENT IN RELATIONSHIPS

Managing anxiety in relationships is like being a skilled dance partner - it requires awareness, communication, and flexibility.

Key strategies:

A. Open communication about anxiety with loved ones
B. Setting healthy boundaries
C. Practising mindfulness during interactions
D. Using "I" statements to express needs and feelings
E. Engaging in shared relaxation activities
F. Seeking support from partners or friends when needed

Interactive Element 4: Relationship Communication Plan

Instructions: Plan to have a conversation with a loved one about your anxiety.

The person I will talk to:

Main points that I want to convey:

How I will express my needs:

[   ]

What support will I ask for?

[   ]

TECHNOLOGY AND ANXIETY MANAGEMENT

"In our digital age, technology can be either a source of anxiety or a powerful tool for managing it. Let's make technology work for us."

Ways to use technology for anxiety management:

A. Meditation and mindfulness apps.
B. Anxiety tracking apps.
C. Online therapy or support groups.
D. Podcast or audiobooks on anxiety management.
E. Relaxation music or nature sounds playlists.
F. Digital reminders for self-care and anxiety management practices

Interactive Element 5: Tech Toolkit for Anxiety

Instructions: Create your personal technology toolkit for anxiety management.

Meditation app:

[   ]

Anxiety tracking app:

[   ]

INTEGRATING ANXIETY MANAGEMENT INTO DAILY LIFE

Name of online support community:

Favourite anxiety management podcast:

Go-to playlist for relaxing:

What digital self-care reminders I will set:

MANAGING ANXIETY DURING MAJOR LIFE CHANGES

Significant life changes can be like massive dark thundery storms for our anxiety. Let's build a sturdy foundation to handle and weather these transitions.

Strategies for managing anxiety during life changes:

A. Maintaining core routines amidst change
B. Breaking big changes into smaller, manageable steps
C. Practising extra self-care during transitions
D. Seeking additional support when needed
E. Using mindfulness to stay present rather than worrying about the future
F. Reframing changes as opportunities for growth.

Interactive Element 6: Change Resilience Plan

Instructions: Prepare for a current or upcoming life change.

The life changes that I am facing:

How this change might impact my anxiety:

Set routines I will continue:

Small steps I can take to help to adapt:

Self-care I will practice:

INTEGRATING ANXIETY MANAGEMENT INTO DAILY LIFE

For support, who can I turn to:

CREATING AN ANXIETY-MANAGEMENT EMERGENCY KIT

An anxiety emergency toolkit is like a first-aid kit for your mind; it is always on hand if needed.

Components of an anxiety emergency kit:

A. Written list of go-to coping strategies.
B. Calming objects (stress ball, fidget toy, etc.).
C. Comforting scents (lavender sachet, essential oils).
D. Emergency contact numbers (therapist, supportive friend)
E. Positive affirmation cards
F. Guided meditation recordings.
G. Calming playlist.

Interactive Element 7: My Anxiety Emergency Kit

Instructions: Design your personal anxiety emergency kit.

Coping strategies list:

1	
2	
3	

Calming objects I will include in my regime:

Comforting scented candles or oils:

Emergency contact numbers:

Three positive affirmations I will use daily:

For guided meditation, I will use:

Songs on my calming playlist:

INTEGRATING ANXIETY MANAGEMENT INTO DAILY LIFE

REFLECTING ON YOUR ANXIETY MANAGEMENT JOURNEY

Assessment and reflection are like a compass for your anxiety management journey. They help you show how far you have travelled, guide you, and ensure that you are heading in the right direction.

Reflection prompts:

a) How has your understanding of anxiety changed?

b) What strategies have been most effective for you?

c) How has managing your anxiety impacted your daily life?

d) What challenges are you still working on?

e) What are you most proud of in your anxiety management journey?

Interactive Element 8: Journey Reflection

Instructions: Take some time to reflect on your anxiety management journey.

1. Write down the three main things you have learned about anxiety:

2. My most effective strategies were:

1	
2	
3	

Chapter Summary:

I know this word has been used many times throughout this book, but I want to congratulate and applaud you! Getting to the end of this all-inclusive step-by-step guide to anxiety management has not been easy, but you have stuck at it, and here you are. At your fingertips, you have strategies and techniques that you can combine with

INTEGRATING ANXIETY MANAGEMENT INTO DAILY LIFE

your daily activities to help you manage your anxiety daily and create a life where you are in control of your anxiety. Your knowledge of how your brain works and how anxiety affects the brain, emotions and body are no longer beyond your understanding. What you must remember is that your ability to manage your anxiety is an ongoing journey, and the skills that you have learned will and should be practised for weeks, months and years to come. While the journey is ongoing, as you practise your skills, management of your anxiety will become a doddle.

Be gentle and patient with yourself. Celebrate your progress and your wins, no matter how small they may seem, a win is a win. You have done amazing work; keep going!"

CONCLUSION:

You have completed "Anxiety Released" Your Anxiety Mastery Roadmap." This is a significant step toward understanding and managing your anxiety. However, this is not the end of your journey. The process is an ongoing journey to management, growth, and well-being.

Continue to practice the strategies and techniques you have learned. Be patient, considerate, and kind to yourself. Celebrate your progress and your wins. Revisit or re-read all or parts of this book whenever you like to clarify or refresh.

You can now create your life where you have power over your anxiety, and your anxiety does not control you. Use your tools regularly and remember your journey and how far you have come.

Your path to a quieter and calmer mind is ahead of you. Look forward and embrace it with understanding, resilience and self-compassion.

"Anxiety Released You can do it!

INTEGRATING ANXIETY MANAGEMENT INTO DAILY LIFE

NOTES

NOTES

INTEGRATING ANXIETY MANAGEMENT INTO DAILY LIFE

NOTES

Make a Difference with Your Review

Unlock Calm for Others

"Sometimes the most important thing in a whole day is the rest we take between two deep breaths." – Etty Hillesum

Thank you for joining me on this journey through *Anxiety Released*. By picking up this book, you've already taken a meaningful step toward understanding and managing your worries. Imagine how sharing your experience might encourage someone else to take that same step.

Would you help someone just like you—ready to ease their anxiety but not sure where to begin?

By leaving a quick review, you're making *Anxiety Released* easier to find for anyone searching for guidance and calm. Your review could help…

…one more friend feel seen and understood. …one more student feel braver in facing their worries. …one more parent find peace and presence with their kids. …one more person reclaim calm in their day-to-day life.

It only takes a minute, but your words could have a lasting impact. To leave a review, simply scan the QR code below. Every review counts in helping others find support and encouragement when they need it most.

Thank you for being part of this journey and for spreading a little more calm in the world.

—Olivia J Patterson

CHAPTER REFERENCES

Chapter References:

Chapter 1: Understanding Anxiety American Psychiatric Association. (2013). Diagnostic and statistical manual of mental disorders (5th ed.). Barlow, D. H. (2002). Anxiety and its disorders: The nature and treatment of anxiety and panic (2nd ed.). Guilford Press. Steimer, T. (2002). The biology of fear- and anxiety-related behaviors. Dialogues in Clinical Neuroscience, 4(3), 231-249.

Chapter 2: The Anxious Brain LeDoux, J. E. (2015). Anxious: Using the brain to understand and treat fear and anxiety. Viking. Porges, S. W. (2011). The polyvagal theory: Neurophysiological foundations of emotions, attachment, communication, and self-regulation. W.W. Norton. Ressler, K. J., & Mayberg, H. S. (2007). Targeting abnormal neural circuits in mood and anxiety disorders. Nature Neuroscience, 10(9), 1116-1124.

Chapter 3: Identifying Your Anxiety Triggers Beck, A. T., & Clark, D. A. (1997). An information processing model of anxiety. Behaviour Research and Therapy, 35(6), 515-538. Wells, A. (2009). Metacognitive therapy for anxiety and depression. Guilford Press.

CHAPTER REFERENCES

Chapter 4: Challenging Anxious Thoughts Burns, D. D. (2009). Feeling good: The new mood therapy. Harper. Leahy, R. L. (2003). Cognitive therapy techniques: A practitioner's guide. Guilford Press.

Chapter 5: Understanding and Managing Panic Attacks Clark, D. M. (1986). A cognitive approach to panic. Behaviour Research and Therapy, 24(4), 461-470. Wilson, R. R. (2009). Don't panic: Taking control of anxiety attacks (3rd ed.). Harper Perennial.

Chapter 6: Mindfulness and Anxiety Kabat-Zinn, J. (2013). Full catastrophe living: Using the wisdom of your body and mind to face stress, pain, and illness. Bantam Books. Williams, M., & Penman, D. (2011). Mindfulness: An eight-week plan for finding peace in a frantic world. Rodale.

Chapter 7: Lifestyle Changes for Anxiety Management Walker, M. (2017). Why we sleep: Unlocking the power of sleep and dreams. Simon & Schuster. Young, S. N. (2007). How to increase serotonin in the human brain without drugs. Journal of Psychiatry & Neuroscience, 32(6), 394-399.

Chapter 8: Relaxation Techniques Davis, M., Eshelman, E. R., & McKay, M. (2008). The relaxation and stress reduction workbook (6th ed.). New Harbinger Publications. Benson, H., & Klipper, M. Z. (2000). The relaxation response. William Morrow Paperbacks.

Chapter 9: Exposure Therapy Abramowitz, J. S., Deacon, B. J., & Whiteside, S. P. H. (2019). Exposure therapy for anxiety: Principles and practice (2nd ed.). Guilford Press. Craske, M. G., Treanor, M., Conway, C. C., Zbozinek, T., & Vervliet, B. (2014). Maximizing exposure therapy: An inhibitory learning approach. Behaviour Research and Therapy, 58, 10-23.

Chapter 10: Anxiety in Specific Situations Antony, M. M., & Rowa, K. (2008). Social anxiety workbook: Proven techniques for overcoming your fears. New Harbinger Publications. Bourne, E. J. (2015). The anxiety and phobia workbook (6th ed.). New Harbinger Publications.

Chapter 11: When to Seek Professional Help American Psychological Association. (2017). Understanding psychotherapy and how it works. APA. National Institute of Mental Health. (2018). Anxiety disorders. NIMH.

Chapter 12: Maintaining Progress and Preventing Relapse Marlatt, G. A., & Donovan, D. M. (2005). Relapse prevention: Maintenance strategies in the treatment of addictive behaviors (2nd ed.). Guilford Press. Segal, Z. V., Williams, J. M. G., & Teasdale, J. D. (2013). Mindfulness-based cognitive therapy for depression (2nd ed.). Guilford Press.

Chapter 13: Celebrating Progress and Acknowledging Achievements Neff, K. (2011). Self-compassion: The proven power of being kind to yourself. William Morrow. Dweck, C. S. (2006). Mindset: The new psychology of success. Random House.

Chapter 14: Integrating Anxiety Management into Daily Life Gilbert, P. (2009). The compassionate mind: A new approach to life's challenges. New Harbinger Publications. Hayes, S. C., Strosahl, K. D., & Wilson, K. G. (2016). Acceptance and commitment therapy: The process and practice of mindful change (2nd ed.). Guilford Press.

Printed in Great Britain
by Amazon

cb917cd7-ee8c-4195-8df4-dfb5c05b5552R01